Dear Knausgaard:
Karl Ove Knausgaard's *My Struggle*
—KIM ADRIAN

A Cool Customer:
Joan Didion's *The Year of Magical Thinking*
—JACOB BACHARACH

An Oasis of Horror in a Desert of Boredom:
Roberto Bolaño's *2666*
—JONATHAN RUSSELL CLARK

New Uses for Failure:
Ben Lerner's *10:04*
—ADAM COLMAN

A Little in Love with Everyone:
Alison Bechdel's *Fun Home*
—GENEVIEVE HUDSON

The Wanting Was a Wilderness:
Cheryl Strayed's *Wild* and the Art of Memoir
—ALDEN JONES

I Meant to Kill Ye:
Cormac McCarthy's *Blood Meridian*
—STEPHANIE REENTS

The Counterforce:
Thomas Pynchon's *Inherent Vice*
—J.M. Tyree

Bizarro Worlds:
Jonathan Lethem's *The Fortress of Solitude*
—Stacie Williams

Looking Was Not Enough:
Jeffrey Eugenides' *Middlesex*
—Irena Yamboliev

THE WANTING
WAS A WILDERNESS:
Cheryl Strayed's *Wild*
and the Art of Memoir

Alden Jones

FICTION ADVOCATE

New York • San Francisco • Providence

A Fiction Advocate Book

The Wanting Was a Wilderness:
Cheryl Strayed's *Wild* and the Art of Memoir
© 2020 by Alden Jones
All Rights Reserved

ISBN 978-0-9994316-6-5

FICTION ADVOCATE
New York • San Francisco • Providence
fictionadvocate.com

Published in the United States of America

CONTENTS

Maps 1

This is Not the Book I Sat Down to Write 18

A Normal Person in the Wilderness 21

The Genre of Our Times. 27

Fashioning Persona 34

My Own System(at)ic Oppression 45

You Construct the Map After You
Have Walked the Land 63

Brave is a Decision 71

Truth Works a Trip Wire 84

Then There Was the Real Live Truly Doing It . . . 104

Boots on the Ground 111

A Note on the Construction of this Book. 120

The Crew. 122

The Urge to Revise the Past 133

Accountability in the Redemption Memoir 137

Fake It 'Til You Make It 148

False Ending One: Love Wins 158

False Ending Two: In Search of Reluctance 168

The End of the Trail 173

References 187

MAPS

Wild is a memoir that begins as a map. Before words, the reader of *Wild* is offered a visual narrative set along the western United States coast. A dotted line extends from Mexico to Oregon, identifying a famously difficult hiking route called the Pacific Crest Trail. Where the dots are blackened in as lines, we see the journey taken by the memoirist, Cheryl Strayed. We envision the trail she followed—alone, on foot.

On its surface *Wild* is the simple story told by the map. Cheryl Strayed sets out to hike a trail, and she achieves her goal. Inspiration, in the form of physical endurance and a test of human will, is the book's very basic premise.

Layered underneath this primary story are the stories about where Cheryl's mind and body have been, and what brought her to the trail: Cheryl's life has fallen apart after the sudden death of her young mother.

She's hit rock bottom, wrecked her marriage, dabbled in drugs, and is on the brink of "ruining her life." Her mission while hiking the Pacific Crest Trail is not just to finish what she'd set out to achieve physically, but to redeem herself. The existence of the book and the fact that you are holding it in your hands proves that she succeeded in the goal of "fixing her life" as well. She has survived; she has become a writer; she has "done well."

These tandem success stories yield a memoir that has become both a rampant source of inspiration and a great literary success. *Wild* was adapted for Hollywood film starring Reese Witherspoon and Laura Dern. Oprah rebooted her book club with *Wild*. The success of *Wild* is so extreme, in fact, that it catapulted its author into the kind of fame that seems, to authors of noncommercial, "literary" fiction and memoir, like winning the lottery.

There are multiple factors beyond the narrative of *Wild* that account for its reach. The Hollywood and big media exposure were, of course, transformative. Strayed had also, in the years leading up to the release of *Wild*, amassed a devoted following as anonymous advice columnist "Sugar," writing (without pay) for the online magazine *The Rumpus*. Curiosity around this mysterious Sugar, with her wise words and frankness about her own hard times, had crescendoed. The dramatic reveal of Sugar's true identity came just before the release of *Wild*. Thus when *Wild* appeared, Strayed was held up as a sage cultural figure, an advice-giver, and the memoir served as an illustration of how she achieved her wisdom. Literary culture holds the story of Cheryl Strayed blossoming from a struggling writer to a famous and successful writer, and *Wild* being the thing that is known for making her famous and successful; this perpetuates the book's appeal.

The glamour of *Wild*'s success must be mentioned. But in this book, I would like to stay close to the text for the most part and examine the nerve *Wild* struck on a personal level that made so many readers feel it was a book that could both reflect and affect their lives. I find this memoir particularly interesting as a case study because the primary story, the account of the hike, of getting from point A to point Z, is itself not all that compelling when freed from the narrative structure. Unless you are a hiking fanatic—and even if you are— hiking as an act is not very interesting to read about. Nothing outwardly shocking or profound happened to Cheryl on the PCT; she did not have to saw off her own arm to free herself from a rock trap or watch people die in a freak storm. And yet, Strayed did something magical with structure and voice and reflection to transform a moderately interesting topic into a memoir *The Boston Globe* called "An addictive, gorgeous book that not only entertains, but leaves us the better for having read it."

Turning a critical eye on *Wild* is not like turning a critical eye on a complex novel. *Wild*'s power is mostly about the psychological response of its readers. It's a story of one person's self that illuminates the reader's own stories of self. Personally, I had a response to Strayed's nonfiction, including the work that preceded *Wild*, that was both personal and critical. Her words on grief triggered a kind of self-forgiveness I had been in search of for a long time. Critically, and as a writer, it became a compelling example of how to build a powerful story out of material that is not inherently narrative.

My introduction to the work of Cheryl Strayed was her 2002 essay "The Love of My Life." I discovered this essay about ten years after it appeared in *The Sun*, right around the time of *Wild*'s publication, when I was experiencing a divine slice of life: my first book had recently sold, my second book won a contest directly on top of that; I was on leave from teaching for the home stretch of my second pregnancy, loving every minute of pregnancy and relishing the time with my young son. My marriage was stable, if not emotionally fulfilling, and we lived in a beautiful home overlooking the Arnold

Arboretum in Boston. In the family room, gazing out over this carefully sculpted green space, while my son was at school and I had nothing to do but wait for my baby to be born and to read and to write, I flipped the page of the anthology I was previewing as a possible textbook for future creative nonfiction classes, *The Touchstone Anthology of Contemporary Creative Nonfiction,* to Cheryl Strayed's "The Love of my Life." Within a few pages I felt as if a warming blanket had been yanked from my body. My present reality fell away; the slider on my timeline bumped abruptly to the left and a decade into the past, and I was dropped into one of the darkest stretches of my life.

I was just past thirty at that time, way too old to fall apart over a breakup I always suspected was coming, but I'd fallen apart anyway. For two years I'd wallowed in a wrecked state. Since my life had improved, I'd worked hard to forget about this painful and too-long episode of grief. "The Love of My Life" brought all of it back, and then did something with it I had given up hoping would happen.

One of the most troubling things about that low episode was that I couldn't forgive myself for having fallen apart. Why hadn't I had a "normal" break-up mourning period, picked myself up, dusted myself off, and moved on? I was angry with myself for the time I wasted, the bottles of wine I drank, the friendships I taxed, the *Law&Order SVU* episodes I watched back-to-back-to-back, the jobs I half-assed, all the embarrassing ways I behaved while feeling so stupidly, hopelessly sad. As I sat with "The Love Of My Life" propped open in front of me I realized I had still not forgiven myself. And this essay, with its friendly, authoritative voice, was a release valve that appeared out of nowhere. I felt like someone had reached through my skin and touched a finger to my heart and then explained the most bewildering emotional state I'd suffered with burning clarity.

The confidence with which Strayed analyzed her own grief following the death of her mother made me feel that I could finally understand myself during my own stretch of grief. I admired Strayed's crystalline prose, her self-knowledge, and her wisdom. I also admired her frankness about what she considered her bad behavior around sex and drugs and even hurting others, and her ability to both own what she had done and forgive herself for these things. On top of being honest with her mistakes, Strayed had an edge. But what struck me most was the authoritative evocation of her empathy. As if she *demanded* empathy, not by issuing a demand, but by rendering its value with such clarity.

When I subsequently came to *Wild*, I assumed this particular grief, the loss of that relationship that leveled me beyond comprehension, was the closest thing I would have to compare to Strayed's mourning, and that this connection would be my way into the book. But when I opened *Wild* and started down the trail with Cheryl, it was a different segment of my memory accordion that flattened out and became real and present after years of my holding it at a distant blurriness.

I held a map. Every day we put our hands and fingertips on this laminated old military issue map of western North Carolina. I stood stalled on the trail with thirteen other people. All but two of us had only a vague idea of where we were: we were lost in the woods, again. Our socks, our hair, our packs were soggy with rain. The two people who knew our exact location were the group leaders. Their job was to empower us by letting us solve our own problems, but they were just as ready to make camp as the rest of us. We looked up at them, pleading: *just this once, help us find our way.* Our leaders tightened their lips into lines. The rest of us hated them, hated each other.

We all wanted the same thing. We wanted to stop walking. We wanted to rest. We wanted to sleep. We would soon be out of daylight, and we'd been hiking in the dark so frequently due to being lost that we had collectively drained our flashlight batteries and were down to four or five shared headlamps for the group, making nighttime hiking over rocks and tree roots unsafe. I didn't dare sit down as we tried to pinpoint our location on the map. If I sat for even a minute I was sure to fall asleep on my pack.

"I think we should turn back and go to the peak where we definitely knew where we were," I said, worried another wrong turn would push us even further into the wooded unknown.

"Fuck you, Alden," said Peter, the boy I sometimes secretly made out with and who was usually nice to me. "There is no way I'm turning around and wasting daylight and energy."

Tears sent streaks of dirt down my cheeks. The next day Peter and I would go back to making each other laugh, and in our group, crew members swearing at each other was par for the course. It was no big thing, but I cried because I had never known this kind of tired and I had no strength to hold in even a small wave of feeling. The wires controlling Peter's filters had similarly been clipped. On the trail, I'd experienced many moments of surprise, observing my limbs or my voice do things my survival-focused brain had no power to prevent.

I dropped the map in the dirt and limped away to continue crying. Someone picked up the map and led us, we prayed, down the correct route. We made camp. In the morning we broke camp and did it again. I was nineteen. I had never known this particular kind of hunger in my life: the actual hunger for food, accompanied by a fear there would not be enough food. Other hungers I was familiar with. They were there with me too, but real hunger and true exhaustion and physical fear came first during those eighty-five days I spent in the wilderness.

Cheryl Strayed's story is about wanting something very specific she would never again have. I had a different wanting and my own wilderness, but it sent me, like Cheryl, into the actual wooded wild, where the feelings spilled over and then lay there in the dirt in front of our boots, forcing us to observe them, and then figure out how to clean them up.

* * *

Almost a decade after I returned to civilization after those 85 days I spent in the wilderness, I found myself in the isolation of a writer's studio at the Vermont Studio Center. I was attempting to write a novel that should have been a short story, but all I knew for sure at the time was that I was experiencing little joy in the act of writing. By my third week I was taking a lot of breaks and luring other artists to the closest café to procrastinate.

My favorite writer to distract was Charles Bock, who was working on a novel partially based on his time as a teenage runaway in Las Vegas. As Charles and I sipped drinks at the café and I listened to him talk about his life on the streets, memories unraveled concerning a girl I'd known who'd also lived on the streets, though under different circumstances. This girl was the sister of someone I'd grown close to during the three months I'd spent off the grid, in the woods. Melissa. (Black hair, black boots, short, muscled, strong—remember this name, Melissa.) In her late teens, Melissa's younger sister spent weeks sleeping under bridges and panhandling for food money. Perhaps she wanted to try out being someone other than who she was: a young, protected hippie from Indiana with nice, professional parents and a large, well-kept home. In my opinion at the time, and particularly now in light of Charles's stories of his youth, this girl's pretense that she had no choice but to live off the kindness of strangers seemed an affront to people who truly had no sense of permanent shelter, and to young people who were escaping situations worse than living on the streets. But there was also the question of her situation that struck a chord with me: What is the appeal of turning one's back on the safety and comforts available to them? What is it we are trying to learn by choosing to do something hard that we didn't really *have* to do?

Because I had kind of done that, too.

In a blitz of inspiration, I returned to my studio and churned out more pages than I had in weeks. The prompt of this faux-runaway I'd known turned out to be a mere lead-in to the bigger story, the one about my long stretch in the wilderness. Eventually I excised Melissa's sister from the narrative entirely. But ruminations on the way some of us check out of structured life, despite our privilege—or maybe exactly because of it—remained.

It was easy to write about my time in the wilderness as fiction. I wasn't really talking about *me*. The story, "Flee," came out so easily and the writing process was so enjoyable I worried it couldn't possibly be good. But I also knew it was good. It became the final story in my second book, *Unaccompanied Minors*. It was adapted as a short film by the Emerson College film department. At the film screening I sat in front of the actress who did not know the character she'd played was based on me;

as far as she knew, Zoe was a made-up character from a work of fiction. It was difficult not to turn around and blurt it out to her.

But of course, Zoe was also very much *not* me.

I'd written a lot of invented plot points into "Flee." Nothing externally dramatic had happened in my personal experience. I manufactured a conflict and climax for "Flee"—a nut allergy; a near-death. Aside from plot considerations, there were other reasons it didn't occur to me to render my wilderness journey as truth. About my lived experience I had no statement to make, other than the vague and expected: "An 85-day wilderness expedition was really hard and made me a better person." The revelations, the moments of triumph, seemed too trite for literature. My crew mates and I would seem too proud of ourselves if I tried to reinvent us without irony, without making fun of us. And since we often behaved badly, exaggerating our shortcomings came easily in fiction. I created an altered version of the organizational parameters that brought fourteen people together for 85 days in the wilderness: I made it a recovery program, a last-ditch effort to turn around teens with a history of destructive or self-destructive behavior. I developed a cast of characters who acted selfishly, bickered endlessly, and who refused for a long time to get with the program. Which, as far as that last part goes, wasn't so far from the truth.

It's just that wasn't *all* there was to us. Why were the flattering parts of us, our epiphanies, our triumphs, the way we supported and loved each other, so difficult to conjure as truth?

There were also logistical plot challenges. The acts of breaking camp, making camp, and walking walking walking would be so boring, so redundant, I thought. To recount it would be so personal, even to the point of self-indulgence—I couldn't imagine anyone who hadn't been there would care.

Yet Strayed did it with *Wild*: she wrote a page-turner about the simple act of putting one foot in front of the other.

How, exactly, did she do it?

I started writing this book to find out.

* * *

Wild begins with a map, and then drops us somewhere unknown along its dotted line: we are in the middle of the story. Cheryl, alone on a mountain slope, several weeks into her trip, removes her boots to relieve her feet. Her backpack pitches over and lands on her boot. The boot flies over the edge of the ridge where she sits, then bounces out of sight. Anyone who's attempted even a day of hiking feels her panic as she watches her boot disappear into the impenetrable brush below.

This is a reliable trick of storytelling: start in the middle of the story; drop us into the heart of a conflict, a problem, and force the reader to consider how the narrator got there, and what she will do next. How will Cheryl—alone, surrounded on all sides by trees and brush, no REI in hundreds of miles—hike with only one boot?

In recounting this moment of crisis, Strayed offers a key to the whole package of *Wild*. *Wild* is the memoir of an unprepared hiker who took on a very, very difficult trail, alone, and while female. The bare foot indicates that physically, Cheryl will suffer pain, and probably terror.

It introduces us to Cheryl's grit. The fact that Cheryl, when faced with the ridiculous prospect of hiking with one boot, then chucks the other boot over the ridge, shows us that we are about to take a journey with a gutsy woman. Perhaps we will become gutsier by our proximity to her.

The fallen boot also serves as a metaphor for the loss of her mother. The boot's loss is sudden and paralyzing. When one boot is lost, what becomes of the other? One boot without the other boot "is nothing. It is useless, an orphan forever more." This is Cheryl's precise internal conflict.

Wild is a hiking adventure narrative; it's a trauma memoir; it's a story of self-reliance; it's an inspirational memoir of overcoming grief. I will look at where *Wild* lands in the greater context of travel or wilderness memoirs, some biographical background, and Strayed's process of envisioning and writing *Wild*, which Strayed has discussed in interviews.

If the primary power of *Wild* is in the emotional response it provokes, the idea of persona deserves a particularly close examination. A memoirist's persona is but one version of the self. The self Strayed evokes in *Wild* is a character many readers—whether they have suffered a major loss or not; whether they have ever hiked or pursued sex or heroin as an antidote for pain or not—can attach and relate to. What does it take to create that appeal, or that writer-reader camaraderie?

A look at Strayed's early essays, "Heroin/e" and "The Love of My Life," both published over a decade before *Wild* came to print, tells us something about how Strayed refined her persona between the earlier essays and the essay that grew into *Wild*. (To differentiate between the author and the character in her nonfiction work, I refer to Strayed as the author and Cheryl as the persona or narrator.) Though these essays, according to Strayed, were not the basis of *Wild*, they offer an interesting look at how a writer's "genesis story," as Strayed has referred to the death of her mother, carries though her nonfiction oeuvre, and how her voice unfolded after years of probing the same material. ("You could fairly well say she was my subject," Strayed writes of her mother in the introduction to *Best American Essays 2013*, "though obsession might be a more accurate word.")

Any travel writer can tell you that a story of a journey is almost never best told in chronological order beginning with the day of arrival. Though *Wild* is purportedly a hiking travelogue, it takes over fifty pages to arrive at the trail. I will look at how Strayed manufactures anticipation, creates a "mission," and weaves memory into action in order to give this story its texture and allure.

It is one thing to say a book is "good" or skillful or excellently written; it's another thing to *love* a book, and many smart readers feel this way about *Wild*. (People tattoo lines from this book on their body.) Strayed uses the specifics of her personal recollections to arrive at an emotional universality the best memoirs achieve. Her voice expresses truth simply, is direct without pandering to the reader or trying to impress with clever lexical tricks. But she also takes risks with the reader in describing her questionable behavior during her grief and instructs us in the procedure of forgiveness.

My goal in *The Wanting Was a Wilderness* is to demystify the memoir-writing process by scrutinizing the mechanics of this excellent and beloved memoir called *Wild*. The exercise: writing, within an analysis of *Wild*, my own narrative diagram of my time in the wilderness, using *Wild* as springboard, mirror, map.

My wilderness experience was not a solo endeavor. My specific challenges were different from Strayed's. But I know something about the way leaving your life and civilization behind—only for a short time—offers an opportunity to change the direction of your life.

THIS IS NOT THE BOOK I SAT DOWN TO WRITE

The book you are now reading is not the book I sat down to write. When Fiction Advocate approached me about writing on *Wild* for their Afterwords series, I projected a kind of extended work of straight criticism, with some of my own stories of the wilderness woven through the critique, fueled by the hazy notion that these twinned narratives would together offer a common statement about the powers of hiking a trail to improve one's character. But just as I crossed the word count marking the midway point of my original vision of the book, I faced a massive life upheaval: the end of my 7-year marriage. That marriage, stable as it was in many ways, had reached a level of personal disillusionment that was suddenly unbearable—both for me and for my wife. But still its unknotting came as a shock. I had come to accept that you could live for many years in an unfulfilling marriage if your logistical concerns were met, particularly if you had young children, and I had steeled myself to live like this, emotionally bereft but functional, because the logistics of raising young children blotted out the priorities of personal need.

My children were one, two, and five. The actuality of dissolving the family unit flooded me with panic. I put this book aside and turned my attentions to legal matters and finances and the emotional fates of my vulnerable kids. I spent a lot of time walking in the Arnold Arboretum with electro-industrial music blaring in my ears, chanting over the noise, "Just keep walking." Steeped in *Wild* when the break occurred, I knew that to keep walking was good advice. I also sensed that this careening life turn and my immersion in *Wild* and the book I was writing about *Wild* had more to do with each other than I understood. When the waters calmed and I returned to the writing of this book, I wrote in order to makes sense of these connections.

The Wanting Was a Wilderness continued to be, as I picked up where I'd left off, a book about how being in the wild can offer you an opportunity to change or understand your life. It is still, at times, a work of straight criticism, both of *Wild* and of the craft of memoir writing. It came to be other things, too. It came to be a book about how reading a book can change your life. It came to be a book about how where you are in your life determines the kind of book you are going to write. Ultimately *The Wanting Was a Wilderness* is my own memoir.

Though my critical lens remained more or less steady from the beginning of the writing process to the end, dismantling *Wild* and using it as a map to write my own memoir became a different exercise in the wake of a life upheaval. Being at a crossroads is exactly the situation "Sugar" specialized in helping to make sense of. *Go ahead*, my author-ego said, as I looked ahead at the path I needed to cut in order in finish the journey of writing this book. *Use the tools in your pack. Figure out how this job must be done by doing it.*

Cheryl Strayed carried duct tape in her pack. She wrapped it around her boot-freed feet. She kept walking. What do you have in your pack? What did I have in mine?

A NORMAL PERSON IN THE WILDERNESS

W*ild* is a memoir in keeping with a long tradition of wilderness writing, but with a twist. The twist—and the hook—is that Cheryl is just a normal, average person who has no expedition experience and embarks unprepared. She is a person who buys a camping stove and fuel and sets off alone on the trail without testing her stove, who is then obliged to swallow cold food because she's purchased the wrong kind of fuel.

The American literary canon is filled with nature stories, adventure stories, hiking stories, and out-in-the-wild memoirs. Traditionally, these stories are told by experts and pioneers. They are, of course, mostly the stories of men: Henry David Thoreau; John Muir; Jack London; Ernest Hemingway; John Krakauer; Paul Theroux. But women, too, occupy space in the literary adventure and nature landscape: Mary Oliver; Karen

Blixen; Lucy Bledsoe; Annie Dillard; Terry Tempest Williams; Camille T. Dungy; Rebecca Solnit.

The traveling wilderness stories most embedded in the canon are mainly those of risk and/or extreme situations. A story like John Krakauer's *Into Thin Air* is, for most of us, an armchair experience; most readers do not expect we'll hike Everest, even if *Into Thin Air* inspires a fantasy of doing so, and we hope we would never find ourselves in Krakauer's situation, ascending a mountain with new acquaintances one day and learning several of them have frozen or fallen to their deaths the next. Reading high-stakes adventure stories is a sustained adrenaline rush by proxy.

Quieter, more contemplative wilderness writers, the Muirs and the Williamses, appeal to readers who find comfort in the natural world. Personally, even though I've lived briefly in Vermont and enjoy camping as long as someone else does the planning, I've always found those "nature writers" alienating. I feel a certain amount of inferiority, reading them, for preferring an urban life. Those naturalists and their followers have the scent of religious zealots: I suspect they are most appreciated by the previously converted.

Wild exists in opposition to these traditions. It's the tale of a normal person in the wilderness, someone who probably doesn't know much more than the average reader about camping gear, safety, or how to cope with crises as they arise. A reader can enter *Wild* as a hiking insider, as someone who already feels comfortable in nature, in order to enjoy the specifics of a particular expedition. A reader is equally invited into Strayed's story, if not more so, if they have never strapped a foot into a hiking boot.

Strayed was not the first person to take this position in memoir. One notable precursor is Bill Bryson's 1998 memoir *A Walk in the Woods*, the tale of a regular guy and his regular-guy companion hiking most un-expertly along the Appalachian Trail. The objective of *A Walk in the Woods*, like all of Bryson's work, is to be an informative guide, useful to someone wishing to visit the territory he describes, with a narrative hook that hangs on Bryson's sense of humor. The high potential for foible is presumably how Bryson chose his expedition companion: a friend who was out of shape, unprepared for the terrain, and certain to say inappropriate things. This approach to narrative—it must entertain above all, and it must harbor conflict along the way—opened the travel story to those who might have only minimal interest in the specific physical space.

The difference between Bryson and the other travel writers being published and featured on the shelves in the late 20th century was personality. It seemed to me that in order to call yourself a "travel writer" in that era, it was necessary to emphasize how much you *knew*. There was a certain amount of didacticism or point-blank talking down expected in the genre. Bill Bryson disrupted this hierarchy by presenting himself as a familiar character, someone smart and skilled at research, but also at ease with himself and his own flawed humanity. Bryson tempers his educational mission with a humor that he is equally able to turn on himself as anyone else. Two decades later we are accustomed to the flawed, even self-deprecating, narrator of memoir. But while Strayed was on the trail on the Pacific Coast in 1995, the genre of memoir as we understand it in the 21st century was in its infancy, and a travel memoir in which the objective was to display all you did *not* know was unheard of.

More common at the time was the style of know-it-all meanie Paul Theroux. Theroux's contract was direct: He would educate you, but not for a moment should you consider yourself his equal; he was more worldly than you, he was smarter than you, he could hike faster than you—and that was why he was the one who'd written the book and you were the one reading it. His writing is full of useful information, but he seems to dislike the tourists, the natives, and probably *you*, the reader. I gathered, in the 1990s when I was starting out as a writer, that I was expected to aspire to be like Theroux if I wanted to be a travel writer. But I found no way to experience his work except from a dry, intellectual distance.

Reading *Notes from a Small Island,* I discovered that Bill Bryson might feel the same way, while also pointing out a crucial difference between himself and the Therouxs of the day. Bryson describes a hike both he and Theroux took in England, one Bryson found humbling: "It is twelve miles from Lulworth to Weymouth. *In Kingdom by the Sea*, Paul Theroux gives the impression that you can walk it in an easy lope and still have time for a cream tea and to slag off the locals, but I trust he had better weather than I. It took me most of the day." It was a subtle but direct jab. What a relief that someone was finally acknowledging the superior positions assumed by writers like Theroux, and to suggest that sometimes travel writers exaggerated their expertness or left out the parts of the story that made them seem less extraordinary. Travel writing was beginning to evolve, and character—persona—would soon gain more traction with readers and editors. The travel writing persona would no longer be dominated by the "expert." As the memoir genre evolved, readers became more interested in the parts of travel writers that make us *human*.

THE GENRE OF OUR TIMES

Strayed has stated many times that during her hike she had no intention of writing a memoir based on her experience. Indeed, I'm sure it never crossed her mind in the mid-90s, when memoir was a genre many found questionable, and its list spare. It is not to say the canon did not hold memoirs before the 90s, among them George Orwell's *Down and Out in Paris and London* (1933); Karen Blixen/Isak Dinesen's *Out of Africa* (1937); Richard Wright's *Black Boy* (1945); Ernest Hemingway's *A Moveable Feast* (1964); Maya Angelou's *I Know Why the Caged Bird Sings* (1969); the essays of James Baldwin; Maxine Hong Kingston's *The Woman Warrior* (1976); and Tobias Wolff's *This Boy's Life* (1989). These pre-boom memoirs were widely consumed and assigned as texts, often for what made their subjects academically "topical." But mostly, literary prose writers of the late

20th century wrote and published fiction, even when the content was explicitly autobiographical.

In 1997 Kathryn Harrison's memoir *The Kiss* appeared; this was the moment I marked the tilt. I worked at the time in Subsidiary Rights at the book publishing company Farrar, Straus and Giroux. When you work in book publishing you have access to paper galleys—"Uncorrected Proofs" in paperback form for the house to deliver to potential reviewers while the book is in its final edits—months before books are released, and it was common practice at FSG to swap galleys with associates at other publishing houses. No one could get their hands on the galleys of *The Kiss*. Everyone in and contiguous to the New York publishing world was reading it and gawking about it: Harrison was a writer people knew. Her three novels had earned her a solid literary reputation. And now she'd authored a memoir about the sexual relationship she had entered into with her biological father when she was in her twenties.

The dominant sentiment around memoir at the time was expressed by the editor in the office next to mine in the wake of *The Kiss*'s publication: "It used to be," he said to me, shaking his head, "That if you had an interesting life story, an editor said, 'write about it as a novel.' And we got art. Now editors are saying, 'Oh, you have had an interesting life? Write a memoir.' And now we're getting confessions."

Something was specifically interesting about Harrison's memoir: she had already written the plot as fiction in her first novel, *Thicker Than Water*. The novel had sold respectably. But the memoir was, in contrast, a runaway train. And *The Kiss did* rise above straightforward confessionalism. It was constructed carefully and beautifully—as her novel had been. That Harrison was baring "the truth" of her romance with her own father, in detail, and dreamily, was the greater draw. Not only *can you believe this is true*, but also *can you believe she is actually admitting this*. It was salacious, and readers loved that—more than they loved its parallel salacious plot as fiction. *This really happened*. Because of this hunger for dirty truths, the memoir boom did, as my editor friend suggested, produce a large number of confessions that were *not* artful. Of the many addiction-to-sobriety memoirs of the late '90s, Michiko Kakutani grumbled in the *New York Times*: "[the] lesser efforts were propelled by the belief that confession is therapeutic and therapy is redemptive and redemption somehow equals art." Kakutani pointed to Mary Karr's *Lit* to identify the exception: the memoir that "demonstrates that candor and self-revelation only become literature when they are delivered with hard-earned craft, that the exposed life is not the same as the examined one."

Other breakout memoirs of the nineties were Lucy Grealy's *Autobiography of a Face*, about the author's cancer of the jaw that led to extreme disfigurement in childhood and a series of unsuccessful attempts to reconstruct her face; and Frank McCourt's *Angela's Ashes*, a chronicle of his impoverished childhood in Ireland during which multiple siblings starved to death, about which the *New York Times* declared in 2019 "The book did perhaps more than any other to cement the 1990s boom in memoir writing—and reading." And so early "boom" memoir was aligned with extremity and shock. Shocking content did not exempt a memoir from careful, artful craft. But it did mean that publishing houses might be marketing the content more than the way the story was told.

Because the wave of memoirs that came out in the 1990s was often about such extreme or even lurid life experiences, the genre of memoir had the scent of self-indulgence, self-importance, and overtelling. Memoirists, if they had survived lives more stable and ordinary than the life of Frank McCourt, were asked, why are *you* so important? Why do you think anyone wants to read about *your* life? And yet, readers did want this. "Real" stories soon sold better than novels and short story collections sold; *Forbes* reported that 2012—the year of *Wild*'s publication—was the last year adult fiction outsold nonfiction published by traditional publishing houses, and since then revenues for nonfiction have steadily climbed while those for fiction continue to decline.

By *Wild*'s appearance memoir had a solid hold in the literary landscape, and it had moved away from its associations with confessionalism and shock value. "Memoir is, for better and often for worse, the genre of our times," Sven Birkerts wrote in *The Art of Time in Memoir: Then, Again* in 2008. "The fact of rampant sensationalism must not be allowed to obscure that other fact, which is that recent decades have seen the flourishing of a sophisticated and quietly vital mode of literary self-expression." Readers had grown comfortable with the idea that memoir was not autobiography, and unlike autobiography—one's entire life story—a writer need not be famous or "important" to justify writing a memoir. The reading public, as well as writers who'd mostly trafficked in fiction up to this point, recognized that the memoir genre had structural rules, and that the rules of memoir were not the rules of fiction, though there are common elements of arc, resolution, scene building, and character development. We acknowledged that within these architectural confines, a memoir could be about something small, something contained to a brief period of our life, and that if we had a solid message or point to make, we need not have achieved anything extraordinary or lived through anything harrowing or tragic in order to write a good essay or book.

The writing Strayed describes doing on the trail is the kind of writing I encourage of my travel writing students while they travel: the recording of details, without a story agenda. I advise aspiring travel writers to avoid, if possible, declaring a "story" before they embark or narrowing themselves to one topic. Write down the details of your day, the names of things, all the things you think you are going to remember, like how much things cost and what you ate and how it tasted and smelled and what the tablecloth and the air felt like. Write down snippets of dialogue. Things you felt, especially when these feelings were confusing. Your "story" may emerge much later—in Strayed's case, the story emerged years later.

But one thing has not changed from the early days of memoir, and that is the risk a writer takes by putting herself on the page and asking you to like her enough to travel a long distance with her. In this regard, *Wild* was a slam-dunk example of soliciting a widespread response by writing specifically and personally about her own life.

But also: writing *carefully* about her life.

FASHIONING PERSONA

Cheryl is someone we'd perhaps like to run into while we're out on the trail, someone it would be enjoyable to walk and talk with. While Cheryl remains for the average reader an armchair companion, she also gives us the impression that we could physically do what she is doing. She is not better or smarter than you; in fact, what she is doing on the Pacific Crest Trail, you may very well do more easily. The data proves how successfully she suggested this: the Associated Press reported that after the release of *Wild* the PCT experienced a surge so extreme they had to enact a new permit system to keep traffic to a reasonable level. (Hardcore PCT devotees are the least likely people to be fans of *Wild*.)

If you were to hike the PCT, you would prepare. You would probably carry a lighter, more practical pack than Cheryl. Cheryl invites you to laugh at her lack of preparation as she laughs at herself. As she organizes her gear the night before her expedition, Cheryl realizes she's put herself in a precarious situation by convincing herself she was more prepared than she actually was:

> I was easily someone who could be described as outdoorsy. I had, after all, spent my teen years roughing it in the Minnesota northwoods. My family vacations had always involved some form of camping, and so had the trips I'd taken with Paul or alone with friends….But now, alone in my room at White's Motel, I knew there was no denying the fact that I was on shaky ground.

Paul, her former husband, had previously suggested that she "try a shorter trip first," gently adding, "It's only that you've never gone backpacking, as far as I know." Cheryl responded with indignation. Then she realized, with some surprise, that he spoke the truth: "In spite of all the things I'd done that struck me as related to backpacking, I'd never actually walked into the wilderness with a backpack on and spent the night. Not even once."

Cheryl both introduces conflict into the narrative (she's in over her head and she's going to get herself in trouble—what kind of trouble will it be?) and generates sympathy in her reader (for her vulnerable state). She also shows that she is not afraid to point the finger at herself.

> *I've never gone backpacking!* I thought with rueful hilarity now.... A month ago, I'd been firmly advised to pack my backpack just like I would on my hike and take it on a trial run. I'd meant to do it before I left for Minneapolis, and then I'd meant to do it once I got to Portland. But I hadn't. My trial run would be tomorrow—my first day on the trail.

Famously, her pack is too heavy to lift: "It was exactly like attempting to lift a Volkswagen Beetle. It looked so cute, so *ready* to be lifted—and yet it was impossible to do." Even then she refuses to reduce her load. She realizes the foldable saw is superfluous, yet it stays in the pack. She is determined to both do this hike and make it hard for herself.

Lest we are tempted to judge Cheryl for her lack of reasonable preparation or iffy judgment, Strayed has preceded her departure for the PCT with 46 pages worth of background on her decision to set out for the wilderness semi-prepared: her consuming grief over the death of her mother. Of course she *should* have broken in her boots, sought feedback on her packing list, and probably checked to make sure her stove and fuel were compatible. But haven't *you*, reader, ever exhibited bad judgment when you were in crisis?

Cheryl's crisis might be greater than any crisis you have experienced or it may be on the same level or it may not quite match the level of crisis you can claim. The impression she gives, in any case, is that she would not judge you for the mistakes you have made in an emotional state. This becomes a key element of Cheryl's persona in *Wild*, and perhaps its most important hook: the idea that came to be known as Cheryl Strayed's *radical empathy*.

* * *

Every human being is the owner of multiple identities. In any memoir, the author must fashion a clean persona out of a wide and sprawling self. Choosing a persona as the showrunner for your memoir is akin to cutting a channel through the vast field of your personality and moving only within this slender ditch. How does a memoirist decide which narrow idea of self will best help them tell the story? And the adjacent question: how much of your *self* can you put aside in a memoir, and still be telling the honest truth?

Vivian Gornick distills the idea of persona in her seminal nonfiction writing guide *The Situation and the*

Story (2002). To illustrate persona, Gornick recounts a eulogy she listened to at a revered doctor's funeral. Why had Gornick cared so much more about the doctor while listening to this particular eulogy, which described the speaker's experience as the doctor's student, than the eulogies that preceded it? This time, Gornick understood who *she*, the speaker, was in relation to the doctor; the subject matter only became vivid when she knew *who* was speaking, and what the speaker cared about.

> Out of the raw material of a writer's own undis-guised being a narrator is fashioned whose existence on the page is integral to the tale being told. This narrator becomes a persona. Its tone of voice, its angle of vision, the rhythm of its sentences, what it selects to observe and what to ignore are chosen to serve the subject; yet at the same time the way the narrator—or the persona—sees things is, to the largest degree, the thing being seen.

Gornick emphasizes how difficult it is to sculpt persona, how much "hard work" it is, but that without persona the entire structure of a memoir is in danger of being loose, unfocused and difficult to connect with. This "hard work" is as much psychological as it is technical, as any true persona requires being frank about our identifications:

> To fashion a persona out of one's undisguised self is no easy thing. A novel or poem provides invented characters or speaking voices that act as surrogates for the writer. Into those surrogates will be poured all that the writer cannot address directly— inappropriate longings, defensive embarrassments, anti-social desires—but must address to achieve felt reality. The persona in a nonfiction narrative is an unsurrogated one. Here the writer must identify openly with those very same defenses and embarrassments that the novelist or the poet is once removed from…
>
> Yet the creation of such a persona is vital in an essay or memoir. It is the instrument of illumination. Without it there is neither subject nor story. To achieve it, the writer of memoir or essay undergoes an apprenticeship as soul-searching as any undergone by novelist or poet: the twin struggle to know not only why one is speaking but *who* is speaking.

In the case of the eulogy, Gornick points out that the speaker may have been many other things—a daughter, a New Yorker, a bird-watcher—but for the purposes of the piece of writing she composed, she limits her persona to one band of her identity; she speaks only as an apprentice to this doctor. By identifying the element of self that best serves the story and eliminating most everything else, she clears a path for the story she wants to tell.

Persona, "situation," and "story" make up Gornick's trifecta of successful memoirs. In a lecture at Bennington College in 1987, short story writer Grace Paley declared that "Every story is two stories. The one on the surface and the one bubbling beneath." This is a variation on Gornick's declaration that "Every work of literature has both a situation and a story. The situation is the context or circumstance, sometimes the plot; the story is the emotional experience that preoccupies the writer: the insight, the wisdom, the thing one has come to say." In my work as a teacher and manuscript consultant, I so often ask variations of the same two questions, cribbed from *The Situation and the Story*, that I should have stickers made. "You have a situation, but what are we supposed to make of it? What's the story?" And "You know what you want to say. But what happened to make you arrive at this truth? What's the situation?"

What seems simple and straightforward can be surprisingly elusive when the writing begins. I have an octogenarian student who describes the editorial work we do: "It's like I write everything I want to say on a topic, and you tell me what it means." She exposes the details of why a certain subject is important to her by putting down relevant episodes on paper, and I help her locate her "story" from these details. She has endless situations to call upon, but even when she delivers a message, she isn't always sure what it is. As a result, her early drafts include superfluous information, contradictory ideas, an incomplete or waffling persona. Once she identifies the "story" though editorial discussions, she rewrites the piece, making sure every sentence drives towards this ultimate message. Sound structure is the natural result of knowing all along what you want to suggest—in one's final draft, if not the first.

Other memoirists are so sure of their message that they state it explicitly throughout the work, eliminating any fun for the reader to figure it out for herself or to share the author's experience. They have an idea of their "story" or the statement they want to make: "I adopted a child, and I want to write a book that encourages adoption," or "I worked in public education in X city, and it's in dire need of reform." The work for these writers is the development of scenes, the evidence that supports their ideas, the age-old dictum "show don't tell." It's common, especially but not exclusively in the case of writers who have lived long lives or who have experienced extended trauma, to feel the need to "get it all down," and the result is often pages and pages of chronological summary with little sense of forward thrust. My advice for these writers is to state explicitly what they want to say: the message, the "story," the point. Maybe you write your story in one sentence on a piece of paper and tape it above your work station as a reminder. Then come up with a list of scenes that serve this point or message, the idea you want to leave the reader with. Every scene must build towards the message you have taped above your work station. Imagine a beaded necklace: each scene a bead, carefully designed and whole; only as much exposition needed to string each bead to the next. The "get-it-all-down" writers are faced with the challenge of cutting out material they initially believe is important—usually a lot of it.

Sureness of persona yields a sureness of voice. Clarity is a hallmark of a well-sculpted persona, and an important element of this clarity is zeroing in on the truth you want to tell. "The secret to any voice grows from a writer's finding a tractor beam of inner truth about psychological conflicts to shine the way," writes Mary Karr in *The Art of Memoir*, adding: "Pretty much all the great memoirists I've met sound on the page the way they do in person." My impression is that what you see on the page is the Cheryl you would come to know in the world. Her persona, rather than something she is hiding behind, becomes a recognizable version of her Self. Matching up these two selves is no easy task for the memoirist, and is a feat in *Wild*.

Many readers I have talked to said the experience of reading *Wild* is similar to a conversation with a good friend. How are so many varied personalities able to access a similar intimacy with the same persona? It has to do with that "tractor beam of inner truth," the self-knowledge and the ability to be clear and forthcoming about it, and what author Steve Almond—the original Sugar and a friend of Strayed's—dubbed the "radical empathy" that emerges from this self-knowledge. The tone of authenticity and self-awareness makes it feel she is being real with you, and that you, in turn, can be real with her, and more importantly with yourself. Almond adds, "We need books, and Cheryl's books in particular, because we are all, in the private kingdom of our hearts, desperate for the company of a wise, true friend. Someone who isn't embarrassed by our emotions, or her own, who recognizes that life is short and that all we have to offer, in the end, is love."

The Cheryl we are introduced to in *Wild* is the daughter of a beloved mother who had scrambled to make a good life for her children and was diagnosed with aggressive lung cancer at age 45. She is a daughter intensely devoted to her mother, who chose to "[fold] her life down" when she learned of her mother's cancer diagnosis. Her "life became unmoored by sorrow" after she arrived at the hospital, just weeks after the diagnosis, to absorb the shock of her mother's death: instead of arriving to see her alive, as she expected, she is greeted by the sight of ice packs perched on her dead mother's eyelids. She is grief-stricken, scooped out, "feral."

From the outset of this hiking story, Cheryl is not claiming any of the go-to identities of Expert or Gear Head or Outdoor Adventure Boundary Pusher. As Grieving Daughter, she leans into her grief, and then she sets out to accomplish something very difficult to help her climb out of grief, all while being unextraordinary. At the bottom of it, she is a Normal Person. Like you. And if you have ever suffered a great loss, she is even more like you.

MY OWN SYSTEM(AT)IC OPPRESSION

I, too, was once a normal person in the wilderness. Though being "not a wilderness person" is not a precise filter through which tell the story of my time in the woods. My persona needs a mission that will drive her towards her "story."

But entering the wilderness physically (and, as you will soon see, psychologically) unprepared is a place to start: I'll place you in the early part of the physical journey, where conflict is clear. But then I will have to go further into the past, to locate a deeper conflict that sprouted earlier.

In September, 1992, three years before Cheryl hiked the PCT, I arrived in the Asheville, North Carolina airport carrying a duffel bag filled with gear similar to what Strayed scattered across her room at White's Motel. Like Cheryl, I was the opposite of an expert or guide. I was technically an adult, and also technically a teenager. There were a lot of things I did not know.

I'd never heard of polypropylene. I'd never used the blade of my Swiss Army knife for anything other than cutting slices off a block of cheese at a picnic. As a kid I'd attended summer camp in North Carolina, where I'd learned to canoe and puncture targets with arrows and jump semi-bravely into a lake crawling with tadpoles, but I'd felt like a misfit there with my Yankee accent, and bewildered as to why my parents hadn't sent me to performing arts camp in New England with the other New York City-area kids.

I was a bookish type who preferred the indoors. I had never been stung by a bee. I was hopeless at team sports. I assumed rain signified the cancellation of any outdoor plans. After growing up in the New Jersey suburbs with the distinct impression that life was more sophisticated elsewhere, I was firmly urban-identified. I had completed two years of college in Providence and arrived on the edge of the Appalachian Trail after a summer in Manhattan. My physical exercise prior to the trip consisted of dancing at clubs and walking between my apartment in Chelsea and my office job in Soho. I considered the Doc Marten combat boots I wore most days the equivalent of "athletic footwear."

I was in Asheville to begin a three-month expedition with the wilderness school of all wilderness schools: Outward Bound. The decision to join this expedition had happened suddenly. I was halfway through college and experiencing a crisis far less acute than Strayed's. I couldn't name it, but something wasn't happening in my life that was supposed to be happening. I'd expected by now I'd feel more like an adult who had conquered some of the childish insecurities I still felt stuck with. I had this notion that I could improve my person in some unidentifiable way.

This is where the persona of my wilderness memoir grows murky. There was no inciting incident that sent me to the woods, no external crisis. I was defined by vague confusion, an identity question mark. I was seeking illumination of some kind, but how can I illuminate a reader via my own blurry lens?

Two pieces of my identity present themselves now, with the self-knowledge acquired over more than two decades, as important at the time: my sexual identity and my academic life.

I've already let you know, through details of my urban orientation and my nonchalance about outdoor activities, that I was not on a quest that had anything to do with the wilderness, specifically. Somehow these two pieces of my identity, which were linked, punted me off my trajectory of college-in-4-years and carried me, voluntarily, into this landscape where I didn't belong.

To understand how and why I will have to search the scenes, fashion the beads for my necklace, the pieces of my history—I will have to mine the memories. I'm going to have to write them down to figure out which ones matter.

Starting with the person I was becoming just before I arrived in Asheville, North Carolina.

I had escaped the gray brick conservative stronghold of my private high school and landed at the liberal-intel-lectual disco of Brown University. For the first time in my life I found myself in the company of large groups of people whose ideological opinions I shared and where I felt I belonged. Growing up I had always felt a little off. I was a shy, fearful, questioning child at the mercy of what people thought and expected of me, confounded on a regular basis by the rules of girlhood in my socially conservative environment. I was insecure and awkward, not quick with wit, and an easy target for mean kids in a world where protections for elementary school kids who got picked on were feeble. I was a slave to the praise of teachers, and I received it most of the time, though gym teachers unanimously disliked me.

Confidence came bit by bit. I survived middle school as a buck-toothed girl in a navy blue blazer adorned with the school seal, talking on the phone with friends for hours before bed, and arrived at high school a full-blown school nerd, almost popular, though still generally considered a little weird. When dating became socially sanctioned I was all in. Curiosity around sex was something I developed exceptionally early—this was part of what made me weird—and by the time my peers were ready to dip their toes in the water, I was pushing back against a dam of great want with all my might.

The certainty around what my body wanted turned out to be a source of solid self-assuredness by the time I reached my early teens. I thought I *might* be smart; it was *possible* I could claim one or two minor artistic talents; but about the pleasure-rewards for living in my body, I was *certain*. I understood this with the same certainty that I would enjoy being pregnant, giving birth, nursing babies, and mothering children; and therefore, despite all the shame inflicted upon girls who expressed curiosity around sex, I knew that at their crux my current urges were sewn seam-tight to those things universally valued about being female. Oddly enough, this assurance made me feel I could relate to boys not as an object, but as an equal. Most girls were not as ready to acknowledge the carnal aspect of their being. Boys were. I was. The sudden open horniness of pre-teen and teenage boys did not disturb me in the slightest. I was glad they were finally catching up.

Because I spent so much time thinking and reading and talking about sex and romance before I entered that world in any physical way, I secured a keen awareness of its related perils early on. Like any fortune hunter, I understood that with adventure came the potential for sabotage. Certain romantic partners were desirable; others were not. It was up to me to choose wisely. There were countless situations to avoid, and many terrible people, all of them boys and men. I considered this part of the deal. It never occurred to me that this deal might be negotiable, that girls and women could demand a different game. I played by the rules assigned, and a skilled player I became. My reward was mostly agreeable, congenial encounters with boys I trusted.

The notion that my class status and a host of other privileges protected me and afforded me this freedom eluded me, since all kinds of nasty, gendered behavior occurred in the "protective" environment of my high school, and those who suffered from it were very much like me on paper. My high school community held many wonderful and caring people, but as in many institutions run by people with money during those Reagan years, the adults in charge often seemed to have questionable motives simmering under their major decisions, and the overarching goal of my high school's administration did not seem to have anything to do with the nurturing of autonomous, mentally healthy young adults. 80s dark-side manifestos like the Bret Easton Ellis novel *Less Than Zero* and the films "The Breakfast Club" and "Heathers" did not translate as parodies to me and my friends; their realms of adolescent brutality and the toxic effects of class privilege were the slightest exaggerations of our reality. Eating disorders and body-shaming were standard for girls, weaponized for boys. Directly outside the high school's administrative offices, boys lined the hallway with hand-made signs and held up numbers to rate each girl who passed by, while the adults rolled their eyes and walked past. There were the sexual assaults I heard about: the classmate assaulted in the woods behind her house by a close family friend who had agreed to walk her home; the friend raped upstairs at a party while I was down in the basement— she told me much later, her voice cracking with shame.

My sophomore year a senior football player was expelled for pinning his long-time friend on a bed, then biting her repeatedly on the chest while she screamed and her friends attempted to pry him off. The only reason he faced consequences was that the group of students had left campus to drink at someone's house, and the assault involved consuming alcohol during school hours; in terms of the bruises on the girl's chest and wrists, his parents claimed in their lawsuit against the school, he had done nothing expellable. Every example of sexual violence was funneled to a specific part of my brain and lodged there, where it mingled with the others— my cache of the worst things that could happen, the cautionary discipline of my sexual education.

In my young mind, the way I'd skirted sexualized intimidation was by having hair-trigger instincts around people and their motivations. I was proud of my ability to remove myself from a baleful scenario or to call a boy out for bad behavior. To win in this world was to be pretty and skinny, smart and athletic, careful and savvy and to not get yourself into trouble. I did my best to check the boxes—I even performed the bare minimum to earn a varsity letter in field hockey—and all the while planned my escape, mostly by doing well in school so I could be as picky as possible about my next environment, which would be, as it was for everyone in my high school class, college. Because my teachers had introduced me to Toni Morrison and Tennessee Williams and the industrial revolution and socialism and Gabriel García Márquez, and because my teachers themselves seemed to come from a more hospitable planet, I understood there were alternatives to this conservative context with its sinister tinge.

But in some ways my ultraliberal college was no different from high school. During my first two years at Brown, a fraternity was investigated for secretly recording sexual encounters with girls who were unaware of the surveillance; no charges resulted. Accusations of sexual assault, some public and some whispered, tore around campus nonstop; men found guilty of assault were frequently sent to live in a different dorm. Beyond the ivory tower, a war began over oil, white California police officers beat Rodney King nearly to death for being black, and Anita Hill was publicly dragged by a room full of almost exclusively white, exclusively male politicians who supposedly represented America. Where I was now, however, I was one of a huge number of people who found all of this unacceptable, who *all* raged against it. My new confidence to express my anger over the fact that where I came from these things were considered "normal," nothing to get upset over, just the way things were, seeped into my relationships from home. And I didn't understand what I could do beyond rage.

Excelling academically would provide solutions, I thought. Diving into books was how I usually figured out the things about life that my immediate context couldn't clarify. I thought maybe I'd like to become a feminist theorist. A comparative literature professor. I enrolled in Accelerated French (so many crucial texts were written in French). I was on my way to becoming a writer of some kind—I'd known this since I was ten. I was accepted into the fiction workshops for which I applied, and rejected for the poetry classes, so I stopped writing poetry and put my creative efforts into fiction. At Brown you had to *try out for everything*, even some classes; there was always the sense of having to prove you were better than other people, which was one part exhilarating (when you "got in"), nine parts exhausting and demoralizing. As for my academic courses...the more I climbed the ladder towards upper level classes, the more muddled I felt.

Things reached a peak when I, an underqualified sophomore, elbowed my way into a senior-level history seminar called Pornography and the Politics of Culture.

"Porno," as my dearest friend Valerie and I first jokingly and then routinely referred to it, was the most over-subscribed history class at the college that semester, and academically I was in over my head, which was I feeling I was growing used to. Ninety-eight students preregistered for Porno. Those who were serious about formally enrolling were to write a letter to the professor explaining why they should be one of the eighteen students admitted to the class. My impassioned case for myself as a pro-pornography feminist landed me a spot, and Valerie was also one of the chosen. Valerie was a right-brained genius who easily digested every text thrown at her in all of her classes. (I will never forget her explaining the maddening philosophies of Thomas Aquinas to me in a way that suggested his work was easy to understand. Not to mention the Old Testament. "What the fuck is up with all this SMITING!" I'd said during my first religious studies class, having been raised an Episcopalian vaguely acquainted only with the love-your-neighbor New Testament teachings of Jesus, and Valerie laughed hysterically and rattled off all the ways the Old Testament God smote people for mind-boggling reasons. "I will fucking SMITE you, humans! I don't care if you touched the Ark of the Covenant by ACCIDENT, I shall now SMITE YOU DOWN!") I had a more methodical learning style, and I'd skipped all the classes expected of the history seniors for whom this class was designed.

I expected Pornography and the Politics of Culture to combine two of my favorite things, academics and sex, but discussions turned out to be theory-heavy, with more talk of "Foucaultian representations of sexuality" than actual sex. I had never heard of Michel Foucault, a shortcoming I understood to keep to myself. I slunk off to the Brown Bookstore and bought Foucault's *The History of Sexuality* and skimmed it in an effort to catch up to the discussion.

We all had massive, nerdy crushes on Professor Dean with her curly red hair and power suits. We nodded along with her every theory on pornography politics, Victorianism, and eroticism, and flew through texts like Walter Kendrick's *The Secret Museum* and Angela Carter's *The Sadeian Woman*, generally agreeing with each other on everything. The Cleis Press anthology Professor Dean assigned but never taught, *Sex Work*, revolutionized everything I believed about the sex industry and sent me directly to Providence's now-defunct feminist bookstore, the Dorr War, where I scanned spines for other books published by this radical press. Halfway through the semester Professor Dean assigned a small helping of anti-pornography feminist theory so we could collectively belittle its faulty ideology. Her straw woman was law professor Catharine MacKinnon, who asserted that all sex was rape and that pornography perpetuated male dominance and violence.

Academic feminism in the early 90s wanted nothing to do with the shut-it-down theories of writers like Catharine MacKinnon and Andrea Dworkin. First amendment activists similarly loathed them for the suggestion that free speech, in the impossible-to-define form of pornography, should be criminalized. Those anti-pornography feminists had legions of smart, far-left enemies, and the Brown zeitgeist leaned hard in this direction. In Porno the senior history majors guffawed their way through the discussion of MacKinnon's *Towards a Feminist Theory of the State*. MacKinnon was repressive, *obviously*, herself anti-feminist by saying no woman had agency over her own sexuality, *please*. (Foucault came up a lot, as an example of someone who knew better than MacKinnon.) But Valerie and I sat silently in class, having privately discussed MacKinnon's more resonating arguments about gender inequality and systematic sexual violence. I wanted to agree with these edgy intellectuals who were smarter and better read than I was. But I did not agree with them.

I agreed with MacKinnon.

All women live in sexual objectification the way fish live in water. Given the statistical realities, all women live all the time under the shadow of the threat of sexual abuse.

A close friend of ours was not leaving her dorm room those days in the wake of disclosing her years-long childhood abuse. There were several active sexual assault cases at Brown involving people we knew. Surviving adolescence and sometimes also childhood burdened by constant sexual threat was something I assumed most girls experienced. Why were these people laughing?

Valerie and I learned MacKinnon's nickname was Kitty so we called her that. We talked about Kitty as if she were a real-life frenemy. She was messing with our romantic lives. And now my self-understanding suddenly seemed even shakier than before.

Women cope with objectification through trying to meet the male standard, and measure their self-worth by the degree to which they succeed.

Suddenly I questioned the authenticity of my desire for boys and men, which was one of the things I'd least doubted about myself for most of my life. I liked being objectified! I enjoyed seducing and being seduced. I loved hard and with abandon, and sex was an arm of that machine of delight. And I had dodged the worst forms of danger, partly via very good luck and the tight-knit social fabric of my upbringing, and partly by possessing a keen and utter certainty of what I liked and wanted and what I didn't and my confidence to express these things. The hot lava core of my sexuality had always been my strongest compass.

But MacKinnon seemed *so certain* that female sexuality was inherently inauthentic, shaped by the oppressive desires of men. I did not, she suggested, actually know what I liked and wanted at all. Pornography, fueled by male supremacy, had decided for me. *The mind fuck of all this makes liberalism's complicitous collapse into "I chose it" feel like a strategy for sanity.* The idea of false consciousness, the willful participation in one's own oppression, immobilized me. Had I been fooling myself by thinking my sexuality *gave me* power? All this time, had I actually been complicit in my own systematic oppression?

Reading Foucault only made things worse. My main takeaway from *The History of Sexuality* was that discourses of sexuality did not reveal what was inherently true about our carnal desires; discourse actually *created those desires* and positioned them as the cultural standard. *They were saying the same thing!* (I could write an analysis of this comparison now and have a ton of fun with it, but at the time it filled the cartoon bubble over my head with charcoal scribble.)

All of this was complicated by the fact that I awakened an acute sexual attraction to women while watching soft-core Showtime erotica with my high school boyfriend, Henry, whom I loved insanely and with whom I had a healthy, intense, and respectful sexual relationship.

Murky persona, indeed.

Late one night, almost summer. My sophomore year of high school, with Henry on his way to St. Louis for college, we hoarded every minute that remained of our time together. We held each other on the scratchy rug, half clothed as the credits rolled. We lived for those rare late nights we were available to each other and the Showtime erotica programming aligned.

After a few exhales that seemed like nervous false starts, Henry spoke. "You *know*," he said cautiously, "You are *really* turned on by those girl-on-girl scenes."

The previous school year, two girls in his class spent what people considered too much time together. Whispers that their relationship was sexual floated through the locker aisles. When either of these girls passed us during free periods, someone—sometimes a close friend of mine—would shudder or shake their hands, as if having accidentally touched something vile, muttering, "Ew, ew, ew." Even the butchest gym teachers in school were tight lipped and closeted. My bulldyke field hockey coach manufactured a crush on the local sports photographer, a basic man with a bushy moustache, after which my fellow field hockey players warmed to her considerably—*phew, I thought she was a lesbian*. Whitney Houston was about to marry Bobby Brown to distract the public from her love affair with her long-time "friend and companion," Robyn Crawford, and then descend into crack addiction. This was the late 80s. Owning queer desire was social suicide. Career suicide. Suicide suicide.

But Henry knew my body, and he knew what my body knew. And I knew too.

"I know," I said, a solemn whisper.

Since he and I knew exactly zero out queer people, this was a colossal piece of information for Henry, but he was not scandalized, and I knew he would keep it between us. The thought of me with another woman delighted him. I had no problem with that. I considered his added excitement one of the best things about this discovery. The notion was new to both of us, and it followed the viewing of whatever Showtime After Hours feature played that night—we were awash in what our bodies wanted. I would not tease it out beyond the ideas of bodies for some time.

What was there to tease out? Oh, yes: as soon as Henry confirmed what I'd already begun to suspect, elaborate fantasies began to unspool about the secret girlfriends I might someday have, the way it would feel to turn towards a girl with undisguised desire. But I was never going to *do* it.

Now you know that I'm going to do it. But I'm going to drop this thread here for now and hope you will sit and wonder about how and where and when I will do it, and what this has to do with my feminist panic and signing up for eighty-five days in the woods.

If you offer your reader just enough suspense to keep them interested, you can jump to an apparently disconnected place in the story. Trust me, reader: I'll return to this.

YOU CONSTRUCT THE MAP
AFTER YOU HAVE WALKED THE LAND

If the story of a hike, of getting from point A to point Z, is not fundamentally interesting, then Cheryl Strayed's artful digressions—the arrangement of demons, memories, mistakes, transgressions, and losses—scattered carefully between the obstacles and victories along the Pacific Crest Trail are what will keep the reader of *Wild* emotionally engaged. The trail becomes the backbone not just of Cheryl's healing, but of her surpassing her persona as Grieving Daughter and Normal Person and transforming into Role Model. The implication, and the inspirational message, stems from the idea that any "normal person" can eventually become her own role model or heroine. *Wild*'s two stories collide in the final chapter when Cheryl reaches the Bridge of Gods, simultaneously completing her hike and reaching a place of psychological acceptance: "How wild it was, to let it be."

It's quickly clear to the reader of *Wild* that the "situation" is the hike itself—the plot, the context—and the "story" is Cheryl's triumph over grief. But by her own account Strayed did not know what her "story" was when she began writing her PCT story. In a Library Talk at the New York Public Library in 2013, and again at the 2015 Chicago Humanities Festival, Strayed described how the process of writing helped her understand where the story actually started and what it was really about.

Strayed felt reluctant to write about her hike, she said, because she "didn't feel it was worthy of literature. I didn't feel that my experience, that adventure, transcended in the way art needs to. I didn't understand that it could be about more than just me and my hike." She knew she had a "situation" in the journey itself. But something was telling her this situation wasn't enough: she had to have something to say about it.

Understanding this need for a message or context—a "story"—she began the book that became *Wild* as an essay, still thinking that she was writing primarily about the physical experience of being alone on the PCT. As she told Paul Holdengräber in a public interview at the New York Public Library, "When I first started writing *Wild*, I distinctly remember saying to my husband, 'I'm so glad I've finally started a book that has nothing to do with my mom.' [NYPL audience laughter.] What was I thinking? I don't even know what I was thinking. It was like I was delusional. I thought I was just somehow going write a book about a hike." In the writing process, she realized that, once again, she had of course been writing about her mother. "Originally I thought I had twenty pages of material on the hike. Then I got to page 80 and hadn't yet arrived at the trail."

Not all memoirists are lucky enough locate their "story" though the act of writing. Sometimes knowing what you want to say helps you figure out where to begin.

But sometimes beginnings come last. A book's introduction is often the last chapter the memoirist or nonfiction writer writes: this is the set-up for the reader, informed by all the writer has learned by writing the book. You construct the map after you have walked the land. This is presumably how Strayed reconstructed her beginning.

With the knowledge gained from the actual writing of the book, where to start the reader's journey? This became a slippery question for Strayed, as *Wild*'s beginning shows. She addressed this difficulty by acknowledging multiple beginnings within the text:

My solo three-month hike on the Pacific Crest Trail had many beginnings. There was the first, flip decision to do it, followed by the second, more serious decision to actually do it, and then the long third beginning, composed of weeks of shopping and packing and preparing to do it....

And then there was the real live truly doing it...

And finally, once I'd actually gone and done it, walked all those miles for all those days, there was the realization that what I'd thought was the beginning had not really been the beginning at all. That in truth my hike on the Pacific Crest Trail hadn't begun when I made the snap decision to do it. It had begun before I even imagined it, precisely four years, seven months, and three days before, when I'd stood in a little room at the Mayo Clinic in Rochester, Minnesota, and learned that my mother was going to die.

Chapter One of *Wild* recounts the days in the hospital and the days after her mother's death, the far-back beginning of her journey on the PCT. In the subsequent chapters of Part One, Strayed uses a bookending technique to maintain the trail as *Wild*'s primary subject matter: she lands us in her room at

White's Motel the day before she sets out, grounds us in the details of her preparation routines, then uses an item of hiking paraphernalia as a trigger for a memory that leads into a flashback.

> I reached into one of the plastic bags and pulled out an orange whistle, whose packaging proclaimed it to be "the world's loudest."… [I] tied it to the frame of my pack, so it would dangle over my shoulder when I hiked. There, it would be easy to reach, should I need it.
>
> Would I need it? I wondered meekly, bleakly, flopping down on the bed. It was well past dinnertime, but I was too anxious to feel hungry, my aloneness an uncomfortable *thunk* that filled my gut.
>
> "You finally got what you wanted," Paul had said when we bade each other goodbye in Minneapolis ten days before.
>
> "What's that?" I'd asked.
>
> "To be alone," he replied, and smiled, though I could only nod uncertainly.
>
> It had been what I wanted, though alone wasn't quite it. What I had to have when it came to love was beyond explanation, it seemed. The end of my

marriage was a great unraveling that began with a
letter that arrived a week after my mother's death,
though its beginnings went back further than that.

Seamlessly Strayed places us even further in the
past where her marriage is failing and she enters into a
rampage of infidelity in the wake of her mother's death.
She goes on to dramatize her half-hearted attempts to
"stop messing around with men" and the realization that
she would not stop; her infidelities would only escalate.
She confesses to her husband; her marriage dissolves. In
the space of three pages she covers a year of her life. She
moves to Portland, Oregon, where she would "leave my
troubles behind, I thought." She ends Chapter 2 on a
cliffhanger: "Instead, I only found more."

With this, she abruptly returns us, in the first line
of Chapter 3, to the motel room on the eve of her
departure.

We trust she will return to the "troubles." She has
cultivated our desire for more information, posed questions to which we now crave answers, and now she can
make us wait.

We're slightly ahead in chronology as Chapter 3
opens—it's the following morning, the day she will take
her first step on the trail. "I showered and stood naked

in front of the mirror, watching myself solemnly brush my teeth." Back in the hiking timeline, we are introduced to The Things Cheryl Carried, all the items, some standard and some ridiculous (the foldable saw), that she'll put in her pack, which, when she bent to lift it, "wouldn't budge." But she was going to have to lift it. Metaphors like this one are sure to lie ahead. "I worked my way through the mountain of things, wedging and cramming and forcing them into every available space of pack until nothing more could possibly fit." Then Cheryl remembers she'll need to fill her 2.6 gallons-worth of water bottles, which will add 24.5 pounds to her load. (The seasoned hikers wince at this number.) At the same time she is doubling down on her cluelessness as a hiker and the unwieldy pack as the symbol for this, she is securing in the reader's consciousness how crucial and scarce water is on the PCT. We'll need this information later, when she runs out of water. Chapter 3 and Part One end as she decides it is "time to go, so I opened the door and stepped into the light."

Wild's Part One determines that the thrust of the "story" will be the quest to swap out her inner darkness with lightness. Strayed has introduced an objective correlative, the object which will hold the emotional weight of her journey: she will carry this unwieldy pack and name it Monster, and she will bear this Monster even as it shreds her feet and twists her knees, but she will keep walking, and eventually she will accept help and purge the items she does not need with the help of a kind trail-mate and her pack will become her familiar companion. Her load will lighten and her body will learn its strength. She will accept kindness and unearth a sense of gratitude.

Object or action triggers will be Strayed's method of disrupting chronology throughout the memoir while maintaining a streamlined, cohesive narrative structure. When we're certain to be grounded on the trail with her, we will go as far back into the scenes of her memory as she'll take us, knowing she will return to the trail. She's careful not to stray too far from the trail with her flashbacks and asides: she's got a mission to complete and we are on this mission with her.

BRAVE IS A DECISION

Early on in Part Two Strayed explains how she avoided the kind of fear that would have prevented her from going it alone on the trail.

It was a deal I'd made with myself months before and the only thing that allowed me to hike alone. I knew that if I allowed fear to overtake me, my journey was doomed. Fear, to a great extent, is born of a story we tell ourselves, and so I chose to tell myself a different story from the one women are told. I decided I was safe. I was strong. I was brave. Nothing could vanquish me. Insisting on this story was a form of mind control, but for the most part, it worked. Every time I heard a sound of unknown origin or felt something horrible cohering in my imagination, I pushed it away. I simply did not let myself become afraid. Fear begets fear. Power begets power. I willed myself to beget power. And it wasn't long before I actually wasn't afraid.

I was working too hard to be afraid.

I could not recognize how much fear ruled my mental condition in the months leading up to my own departure for my wilderness expedition. By all appearances, everything in my life was fine. I loved college and had made great friends. Valerie and I made plans to launch a campus-affiliated literary magazine centering "feminism and women's issues." I sang in a madrigal a cappella group, dated people, went to parties, and spent many social nights studying on the A Level at the Rock, joyful for a wide circle of friends who also enjoyed reading in a library with periodic breaks to discuss our reading material. I knew, during all of this forward motion, that I was harboring some powerful and unhealthy emotions. I recognized them as outrage and frustration and longing. Largely, the psychic dust storm around my deep dive into Catharine MacKinnon and shut-it-down feminism had to do with fear: fear that there was no hope that women could ever walk the world without the constant companion of sexual threat or kept down by sexual politics. Fear that I wasn't as smart as my college peers who could block out the "personal as political" and see everything on intellectual terms; if I'd thought I might become some kind of feminist theorist, based on my experience in Pornography and the Politics of Culture, I was hopelessly in the wrong camp. Not only did I align with the wrong philosophies; I also found the postmodern academic style of the day deliberately unreadable, all the theoretical text titles with their "destabilizing" parentheses converting one word into two annoyingly trendy, and its verbal acrobatics a distraction from the actual ideas. How could I contribute to the conversation when I possessed this outdated notion that reading should be…*enjoyable*?

Now I was also certain I was too afraid to be gay.

Let me explain to you what I looked like at nineteen. Physical self-description is one of the harder things for a memoirist to do. Especially a female American one. Self-deprecation is expected, and too easy—no one will be put off by you if you say you thought you were fat or that something was aesthetically "wrong" with you, even if the photographic evidence suggests otherwise. This is expected of American women and girls. But to state in some unqualified manner that you were attractive is a surefire way to discontinue a reader's sympathies.

I did think I was fat, and the photographic evidence proves otherwise. I had many common afflictions in relation to my physical self-regard. But I was a certain kind of pretty. I was a teenager of average height, average weight, with "child-bearing" hips, and disagreeable belly fat that could, by some but not all, be ignored, with long skinny legs, dark eyes, and long blond hair. At some point during my freshman year I learned I was on Sigma Delta's "top ten" list—one of the ten girls the fraternity brothers had their eyes on, based on the photographs in the first-year "pig book" directory. I was the kind of pretty *frat boys* liked, which is to say, *conventionally*.

This did not make me popular with the queers overseeing the scene at Brown.

Just before the cheerful rainbow flag became the symbol of queer inclusivity, in the 80s and 90s, coming out meant exiting one geography and staking claim in another. This was the era of the pink triangle. Silence equaled death. Americans, young and old, died of AIDS while their government did nothing to address the epidemic. Young queers were regularly cut off from their families and celebrities deadbolted themselves in closets. Queer life was legitimate subculture and you were in or you were out. If you identified as bisexual, wavering back and forth between society and its fringes, you were probably just not daring enough to live out as gay. Perhaps that applied to me, I agonized.

If I were brave, I might reject male domination in the form of heterosexuality absolutely, pleasing both the Catharine MacKinnon who now lived in my head and the queer social overlords with their mistrust of bisexuality. But I still hadn't mustered the bravery to come out at all in any public way.

A flyer tacked to a tree on the quad announced a meeting of a group called QUACO: Questioning and Coming Out. I burned the meeting details into my brain. I chided myself that going to a university-sponsored meeting was a dumb way to come out. Most girls came out by shaving their head and sleeping with a known lesbian or their "best friend."

I had so far slept with one girl. It had been one of the most flustering experiences of my life. The event was orchestrated by the boy I'd just started dating, who had intended it as a threesome. (Of course.) H. arrived drunk at my dorm room and we sat on the carpet remnant between my bed and my absent roommate's bed, talking as H. chain-smoked Camel filters, and then we had tentative sex on the carpet, each of us apparently waiting for the other's instruction. Afterwards, when I saw her, in the dining halls or with mutual friends on the quad, she iced me absolutely. "Hi, H.!" I would cry out hysterically, and she would mutter "hi" and brush past me. I had never been treated like this by a boy or experienced anything of this kind.

A year later H. would arrive once again unexpectedly at my dorm room door, sober this time, and ask to come in. She would apologize and explain that she hadn't known how to act at the time. She'd been sleeping with a lot of people in a self-destructive way. I had clearly not been looking for that kind of encounter, and considered sex-as-self-destruction an alien idea. As far as I'd been concerned I was at her mercy, since she had been with women before and I had not. She'd had no idea what to do with that power. We were friendly after her apology, but in the months after we'd slept together, during which time I'd seen that flyer tacked to a tree, I was utterly shaken. But I was also electrified. I'd crossed a line and owned a new secret life. There was no going back.

On the evening of the QUACO meeting, I ascended the stairs to the second floor of Faunce, heart thumping, and slid into the meeting room. I froze in horror as my foot crossed the threshold. Out of the six thousand undergraduates at Brown there were maybe four or five students who had also attended my small high school. And there, perched on the desk in the position of greeter, was someone I knew from high school: Daniel, the editor of my high school's literary magazine before I became editor.

"Alden?" he asked, his face twisted in surprise.

"Daniel?" The rest of the room grew quiet and stared.

"What are *you* doing here?" he blurted.

Of course Daniel, a fellow former-closeted high school acquaintance, would not rat me out with bad intentions. But now my anxiety had doubled down. There was no pretending I could keep my queer existence a secret much longer. Simultaneously, Daniel's reaction confirmed that queers looked at me and didn't recognize me as one of them. Part of the problem was that I was known to have boyfriends—Daniel had known more than one. But the bigger problem, in the broader social context, seemed to be the hair.

I stood in front of my dorm bathroom mirror and pictured my face without the frame of my hair. My hair ended halfway down my back. It was thick and honey blonde and straight with occasional luxurious waves. No way was I cutting off this hair.

Until the very end of college, whenever I climbed the stairs to the queer-hosted parties on Ives street, the queer at the door taking cash marked my hand with the symbol for Straight, and then smirked at me when I protested. *Sorry, girl. Everything about you says straight.*

How could I square the straight vibe I sent the world with the fact that the rare, explicit lesbianism in *Henry & June* exhausted me with desire so strong that I returned from the movie theater to my dorm room and collapsed on the floor?

I was fiercely queer, I knew; but I also dwelled in a house with an escape hatch. I was attracted to women, but I was also attracted to men; my body understood this to be absolutely true. This meant that I could decamp, at any time, to the safe area of my identity, claim the social benefits of long blond hair, the source of my femininity, the symbol of my straightness. What if my attraction to men really was a social construct I'd embodied, and the thing holding me back from my true life was fear of losing these privileges? Did that snuff out the love I'd experienced with boys in the past—which had indeed felt very real? I agonized over my identity options, trying to understand who I was at my core and how that fit in with who I wanted to be.

My friends, meanwhile, didn't care how I presented or identified. I'd taken a fiction workshop with gay icon Edmund White and started meeting him outside of class for lunch. He was 52, a ground-breaking writer who wrote gay stories for gay people that straight people also happened to read and revere. Ed had come out in a far more hostile time and place, showed little interest in identity politics, and was the kindest, friendliest intellectual I'd ever met. He might drop a comment into the conversation about a tiff he'd had with Susan Sontag in response to my social laments.

"You can be a lipstick lesbian!" he said. Ed didn't care that I both craved gay community and also wanted to have boyfriends. This just gave me more to gossip about and Ed loved gossip. The server at one of the cafés where we met was a friend of mine from classes. "Hi Alden! Is this your dad?" she asked. "No, I'm her professor," Ed told her, adding, "We're having an affair!" He turned to me with his boyish grin as my friend's mouth dropped open. Ed was a paragon of not caring what people thought. But despite the friendships and community I already had, I still felt something inside me was confused beyond resolution.

I did not yet understand Cheryl's idea that bravery was a choice. That you were the only one who could manage the level of your fear. I wanted the world to bend around me. To become, in a snap, a place without homophobia, without sexual violence built into everyday life, where I could have long hair and be attracted to both boys and girls and not want to punch people in the face all the time (the men who'd dragged Anita Hill, for example) because they would stop being people who deserved to be punched in the face. I had no "radical empathy" for myself or for anyone else. I didn't understand how methodically and slowly ideologies needed to be dismantled. I didn't know how to have empathy for people I disagreed with, who were products of these ideologies.

I only knew I was going to have to find a way convert my ferocity into actual strength. Potentially so I could be in a better position to punch someone if I needed to defend myself or righteousness. That was my idea of bravery at age nineteen.

Since I did not understand that I could take the path of learning bravery and confidence for myself, I decided Outward Bound was going to do it *for* me.

At the end of my second year of college, I inquired about the longest organized wilderness programs I could find. But I'd decided to apply too late; all the semester-long Outward Bound and NOLS courses were full. I sublet an apartment in New York with three friends for the summer and worked at the Soho office of PEN American Center as an intern for the Freedom to Write Committee. I became versed in the First Amendment, finally grasped the hitches in MacKinnon's and

Dworkin's anti-pornography activism, and drafted letters to heads of countries urging them to release imprisoned journalists. At PEN, I was surrounded by adults working in a literary atmosphere—many of them writers, all self-assured, whose visions opened up the world to me.

Queers ruled the PEN office. But theirs was not the familiar ivory tower political queerness. My coworkers only cared where you wanted to go after work. My work friends Tyler and Steve adopted me, escorting me to Splash bar and house parties in Chelsea where the men were chiseled and shirtless and wanted to dance with me in the friendliest way. We waited in line for the New York premiere of Greg Araki's "The Living End" with a huge excited mass. I marched in my first Pride parade and no one objected to how long my hair was or that I was wearing a girly, fit-and-flare dress I'd bought off a rack on the street in the West Village. The gays in New York in the 90s knew how to have an uncommon amount of fun. In their company I felt freed.

Invigorated by what I considered a preview of my adult life in New York, I prepared to return to college for my third year. But then a last-minute spot opened on an Outward Bound semester program in North Carolina, Florida, and Mexico. Three weeks after I ambivalently claimed my spot, I boarded the plane to Asheville, North Carolina from New York.

Outward Bound provided a checklist to help us prepare. They wrote, "be able to run five miles without stopping," so I ran every day on the treadmill until I could run five miles a day. They specified the required tools of our Swiss Army knives. They detailed the material of our winter parkas, which we would need for the final leg of the expedition: the ascent of a 17,400-foot volcano, Iztac-cíhuatl, on the border of the State of Mexico and Puebla, permanently covered in snow and glacier.

The most important thing was the broken-in boots. They were on you every day, and there was nothing you would need to rely on more. My boots were light brown leather, fully utilitarian. I chose them because the brand was on the list of Outward Bound approved footwear, and the REI salesperson told me they were the right boots for me. They were ugly, and I never did grow to love them, though I knew I was supposed to love them as I was supposed to love my actual feet.

Had I known more, I could have taken one look at the feet of my companions that first day in Asheville and inferred a great deal of basic information about them based on their boots. Melissa, a small girl from Indiana, wore the boots I instantly coveted. Her black Merrell Wilderness boots were designed for the most intense mountaineering. Melissa's boots were top shelf, though the rest of her look—ripped shorts, hairy legs—was raggedy. They had shape and style and silver hardware against the dark leather. Most of us owned newish brown boots with red or brown laces. Fat bright blue laces criss-crossed Melissa's black Merrells, and judging from the bends in the leather she had owned them longer than the rest of us, yet they still appeared minimally scuffed.

I entered the wilderness with all the proper objects. I was not the kind of person who would buy fuel for a stove without triple-checking that it was the right kind of fuel. But I did not have grit. Melissa with the black boots, like Cheryl with her one boot, and later the shoes she fashioned from duct tape, had the grit. If Strayed's "story" was one of combating an inconceivable sorrow, armed with the grit, mine was the quest for grit, armed with the gear.

TRUTH WORKS A TRIP WIRE

Cheryl Strayed's nonfiction works brim with personal details and the key facts of her biography are well known. There remains a curious time between the point at which *Wild* ends and its publication, and the question of what material Strayed omitted from her life story in *Wild*. Much of the information from this era is discussed in the copious interviews Strayed has conducted. Some can be understood through the essays she wrote during that time.

Cheryl Strayed was born Cheryl Nyland on September 17, 1968, in Spangler, Pennsylvania. When she and her sister and brother were young, her mother left her abusive father and raised them on her own in Minnesota. Eventually, Strayed's mother remarried a man named Eddie who became a father figure to Strayed and her siblings. The family existed in poverty, but "rich in love," and eventually made a home in the woods of Minnesota, where they lived for a while in a tar-paper cabin with no bathroom or running water.

Though she doesn't discuss her high school popularity in *Wild*, Strayed was a cheerleader and homecoming queen. She also, as she mentions briefly in *Wild*, struggled with an eating disorder as a teen. "I don't think that I had full-on anorexia or bulimia," Strayed told *Oprah*. "But I did have a totally messed-up relationship with beauty and my body." Strayed recounts that when in ninth grade, "I just decided that I needed to be that skinny cute thing. So I just stopped eating. By the end of that freshman year, I remember, I weighed in the 90s, and the sad thing was I got all this positive feedback. All the girls my age were saying, 'Oh, you're so pretty. You're so skinny.' Suddenly, I went from being somebody who's this average person to someone whom everyone compares themselves to, and there's a lot of power in that."

Because Strayed gives significant attention in *Wild* to recounting sex and seduction and her unspoken sexual power—not to mention the fact that a walking story is, inherently, a story of the body—this relationship between her body and the world might have been an interesting road for her to go down in the memoir. But to amplify this thread would place emphasis on her relationship with her gendered body, and Strayed clearly did not want this to be the message at the heart of *Wild*.

It would also be a dicey path, for the same reason it is difficult for a female memoirist to describe herself as attractive. Interestingly, Strayed revealed in a panel discussion at the AWP Conference in 2019 that she had originally included in *Wild* "more about" how most of the men she met on the trail had "hit on her." "Not menacingly," she said; "Cheerfully. But I was told that it sounded like I was bragging. Well I didn't want to sound like *that*. So I took it out." What she realized later, she said, was that this "was a way of erasing women's experience."

Strayed does briefly address her role as a sexualized woman, in part by "neutralizing" it, but not entirely:

> I was, after all, what Ed referred to somewhat inaccurately as the only girl in the woods, alone with a gang of men. By necessity, out here on the trail, I felt I had to sexually neutralize the men I met by being, to the extent that it was possible, one of them.
>
> I'd never been that way in my life, interacting with men in the even-keeled indifference that being one of the guys entails. It didn't feel like an easy

thing to endure… I'd been a girl forever, after all, familiar with and reliant upon the power my very girlness granted me. Suppressing these powers gave me a gloomy twinge in the gut. Being one of the guys meant I could not go on being the woman I'd become expert at being among men.… The one I'd banked on all through high school, starving myself thin, playing cute and dumb so I'd be popular and loved. The one I'd fostered all through my young adult years while trying on different costumes— earth girl, punk girl, cowgirl, riot girl, ballsy girl. The one for whom behind every pair of boots or sexy little skirt or flourish of the hair there was a trapdoor that led to the least true version of me.

Now there was only one version. On the PCT I had no choice but to inhabit it entirely, to show my grubby face to the whole wide world. Which, at least for now, consisted of only six men.

Cheryl in *Wild* does have a voice Strayed seems to have *arrived* at by making these and other careful choices, and "from the vantage point of the 40-year-old who knew how it all turned out" (AWP panel 2019). Strayed did not write *Wild* immediately upon unpacking her Monster backpack and resuming her existence in

the regular world. It took many years for her to understand the significance of her hike and its impact on her
life. *Wild* was born of the secure worldview she acquired
after living through years of confusion and doubt.
The book could not have happened without the years
between the hike and the writing of the book about the
hike, that mute time in the loop that remains the most
mysterious element of Strayed's character.

Strayed's early literary aspirations were in the genre of
fiction. She pursued an MFA in fiction at Syracuse with
the goal of writing novels. Her first novel (and only one
to date), *Torch*, was published in 2006. As described
on the book jacket, *Torch* was the story of "Teresa Rae
Wood, a teen mother and an abused wife who escaped
to Minnesota, fell in love, raised good kids," living a
good life and generally "being incredible," "until she's
diagnosed with cancer and learns that she has only
months to live." Ultimately, the "family loses its center
after Teresa's death," and everyone suffers. Teresa Wood
was Strayed's attempt to bring her mother back to life.
Like Kathryn Harrison, Strayed tried out her life story
in fiction before memoir.

Though *Torch* was a solid novel that received some
critical attention, Strayed later wrote that something

about trying to recreate her mother in fiction psychologically backfired. It was about the form, the fictionalizing. "All of that conflating and distilling and mishmashing hadn't make my mother more pure," Strayed wrote. "It hadn't conjured her back into the world. Fiction had ruined her."

Mary Karr explains a phenomenon that occurs when the writer faces up to true events and true beliefs: "Truth works a trip wire that permits the book to explode into being." In her essays and interviews, Strayed describes the initial process of writing about her mother's death as a sort of explosion of truth.

Strayed's first essay—her trip wire—seemed almost to happen to her while she was in Taos as a fellow at the Wurlitzer Foundation in 1997. She was at the residency to work on *Torch*. Her mother had been dead for six years, and "in those six years she'd been dead [Strayed had] written about little else." One morning she woke up at the residency, she writes, "abruptly and tearfully, as if from a nightmare, and sat straight up in bed with the icy realization that I was forgetting my mother." On this morning Strayed turned away from the fictionalized mother, Teresa, and began writing about her actual mother, not as a fictional character "condensed and expanded, magnified and muted, twisted and reformed—my attempt to create the purest expression of who she was," but as the mother she had known.

Strayed writes: "I went immediately to my computer and began writing with one simple mission: to remember my mother."

The essay she began was "Heroin/e."

> When my mother died, I stripped her naked. Plush round belly and her pale breasts rising above. Her arms were black-and-blue from all the needles going in. Needles with clear liquid and needles that only the nurses had a hold of and other needles gripping constantly into her, held tight with tape to the translucent skin of her hand or the silk skin of her wrist. And not one of those needles trying to save her.

"Heroin/e" recounts Cheryl's mother's last days, and also the two women's parallel journeys into pain-numbing opiates: we learn that after her mother received morphine to lessen her pain at the end of life, Cheryl sought solace in heroin after her mother's death. "Heroin/e"'s overall voice has harder edges than the later memoir, though passages from "Heroin/e" find their way into *Wild* almost word for word. There is less of an invitation in "Heroin/e" to share Cheryl's experience and greater intent to pierce the reader with the intensity of feeling. The content of "Heroin/e" calls to the reader's attention something that is notably absent in *Wild*, considering its role in the early part of the narrative: what it feels like to use, or want, heroin.

The first time I smoked heroin it was a hot sunny day in June. I got down on my knees in front of Joe, where he sat on the couch. "More," I said, and laughed like a child. "More, more, more," I chanted. I had never cared much for drugs. I'd experimented with each kind once or twice, and drank alcohol with moderation and reserve. Heroin was different. I loved it. It was the first thing that worked. It took away every scrap of hurt that I had inside of me. When I think of heroin now, it is like remembering a person I met and loved intensely. A person I know I must live without….

I wanted it and I got it, and the more heroin we got, the stingier we became with it. Perhaps if we snorted it, we thought, we'd get higher on less. And then, of course, the needle. The hypodermic needle, I'd read, was the barrier that kept the masses from heroin. The opposite was true with me. I loved the clean smell of it, the tight clench around my arm,

the stab of hurt, the dull badge of ache. It made me
think of my mother. It made me think of her, and
then that thought would go away into the loveliest
bliss. A bliss I had not imagined.

In *Wild*, the impression we get of Cheryl's mother
is that as she closes in on death, she is forced to sink
into pain. In "Heroin(e)," nearly identical scenes are
recontextualized and pushed up against Strayed's
descriptions of her heroin use, leaving the impression
that the mother in "Heroin/e" is sinking not into pain,
but into the oblivion of morphine. The effect is to show
the degree of Cheryl's own psychic pain, a pain like
death itself, and her need to deliver herself from it. Pain
is the end game. But because the thread is explicitly
drug-related, "Heroin/e" becomes a "drug story," with
the narrative hanging specifically on the use and experience of a drug.

Drug stories are difficult to pull off. There are of
course excellent examples of drug stories done well
(Denis Johnson's *Jesus's Son* is a favorite to many). But
there are standard reasons drug stories fail to engage
general readers. To readers apathetic to the idea of a
chemical high, or who see drug use as a weakness or
character flaw, or to whom the idea of using illicit

substances is too far outside their own experience to find personal purchase in a story hinging on such material, drug stories have no floor. General readers are hard on drug memoirs unless they follow the predictable formula of rock bottom to sobriety, assuring the reader with a straightforward anti-drug message. I've noticed undergraduate writing students, with their constant proximity to people acting stupid on mind-altering substances, tend to consider drug stories presented for workshop braggy or self-indulgent, sometimes a display of bad character.

Yet "Heroin/e," first published in *DoubleTake*, was chosen for *Best American Essays 2000*, a solidly mainstream prize anthology. What delivers "Heroin/e" and to a greater degree *Wild* from marginalization is the context of loss and pain that is specific (she suffered due to the death of her mother) and universal (we can all imagine the pain of losing the person closest to us).

Heroin does not make an explicit appearance in *Wild* until page 52. The small and delayed role of drugs in *Wild* carefully avoids alienating a general readership or placing heroin near the heart of the story. The drug first appears in *Wild* in the form of a hint: Cheryl describes a bruise on her ankle. By the time we learn, many pages later, the bruise was the result of shooting up one last time with her bad-boy boyfriend, we've built up our own tolerance: grief-stricken Cheryl has earned our sympathy.

Strayed omits the visceral descriptions of using heroin and plays a more anti-drug tune in *Wild*. Gone are the descriptive odes to the sensory experience of heroin, replaced with Hemingway-esque statements and attention-diverting reminders of her emotional state:

> It was good. It was like something inordinately beautiful and out of this world. Like I'd found an actual planet that I didn't know had been there all along. Planet Heroin. The place where there was no pain, where it was unfortunate but essentially okay that my mother was dead and my biological father was not in my life and my family had collapsed and I couldn't manage to stay married to a man I loved.
>
> At least that's how I felt while I was high.
>
> In the mornings, my pain was magnified by a thousand.

No longer a drug story, *Wild* does not offer the reader even a moment to enjoy (or resist enjoying) the sensation of using a drug. The emphasis is on pain— and this time, reader, you will get your redemption at the end of the story.

As in "Heroin/e," we see in Strayed's subsequent essay "The Love of My Life" the same or similar terrain as in *Wild*, differently framed: the death of Cheryl's mother is at the forefront; Cheryl's persona involves self-destructive behavior, this time as a sexually promiscuous young women who accepts advances from questionable strangers.

The opening line is designed to jolt: "The first time I cheated on my husband, my mother had been dead for exactly one week." She goes on to describe an unpleasant encounter with a man who approached her in a coffee shop:

> He thought I looked intriguing. He thought I looked mature. I was twenty-two. He was older, possibly thirty. I didn't ask his name; he didn't ask mine. I walked with him to a parking lot behind a building. He stopped and pressed me against a brick wall and kissed me, but then he wasn't kissing me. He was biting me. He bit my lips so hard I screamed.
>
> "You lying cunt," he whispered into my ear. "You're not mature." He flung me away from him and left.
>
> I stood, unmoving, stunned. The inside of my mouth began to bleed softly. Tears filled my eyes. I

want my mother, I thought. My mother is dead. I thought this every hour of every day for a very long time: I want my mother. My mother is dead.

It was only a kiss, and barely that, but it was, anyway, a crossing. When I was a child I witnessed a leaf unfurl in a single motion. One second it was a fist, the next an open hand. I never forgot it, seeing so much happen so fast. And this was like that — the end of one thing, the beginning of another: my life as a slut.

If trustworthiness is a characteristic a reader values in a memoirist, Strayed has taken a gamble by opening this essay with her infidelity. She's banking on the reader coming to understand that this blunt admission—blurted out before we even know her—is the ultimate act of coming clean.

"The Love of My Life," like "Heroin/e," is loaded with emotive ammo. The introductory scene is unpleasant, physical, and involves a shady stranger and our protagonist being in harm's way. It evokes unpleasant feelings. This, too, is a risk: not all readers want to feel that way.

The reader is not trapped in this discomfort long, however, because Strayed has split herself in two in "The Love of My Life," much like I have split her in two by referring to her alternately as Cheryl and as Strayed. Instead of offering a narrator temporally stuck in that place where Cheryl was suffering and acting out, and trapping the reader in this space of grief and shame, her persona alternates between the young woman in mourning and the wise narrator of years beyond. She describes her past suffering, and then pulls back to the wisdom of the present, offering a sort of cultural analysis of her condition:

> I needed my stepfather to be the kind of man who would suffer for my mother, unable to go on, who would carry a torch. And if he wouldn't do it, I would.
>
> We are not allowed this. We are allowed to be deeply into basketball, or Buddhism, or *Star Trek*, or jazz, but we are not allowed to be deeply sad. Grief is a thing that we are encouraged to "let go of," to "move on from," and we are told specifically how this should be done. Countless well-intentioned friends, distant family members, hospital workers, and strangers I met at parties recited the famous five stages of grief to me: denial, anger, bargaining, depression, and acceptance. I was alarmed by how many people knew them,

how deeply this single definition of the grieving
process had permeated our cultural consciousness.
Not only was I supposed to feel these five things,
I was meant to feel them in that order and for a
prescribed amount of time.

The authority of the wise narrator, fortified by
a perspective beyond the experience she recounts,
provides the scaffolding for the chaos of her earlier
self. This is the combination of objective wisdom and
no-holds-barred personal disclosure we will later see in
Wild with greater restraint.

In the end, "The Love of My Life" is a story about
excess. This is its main difference from *Wild*, along with
the important fact that Cheryl does not recover by the
end of the essay. "The Love of My Life" was written
against the redemption memoir, and grief extends
beyond the end of the piece. Her grief is excessive: "We
aren't supposed to want our mothers that way, with the
pining intensity of sexual love, but I did, and if I couldn't
have her, I couldn't have anything...I was bereft, in
agony, destroyed over her death." Instead of cheating
on her husband with one or two people, she cheats with
many. And then comes heroin, the most immoderate of
drugs. The voice, with its control and insight into events

of the past, cinches this excessive emotion and behavior into a tight, even uplifting message: Sometimes you can't pull yourself together. Sometimes you have to let yourself be wrecked. If *Wild* is about being lost and then found, "The Love of My Life" is about being lost, not knowing how to get found, and trusting that it is okay to be lost for as long as you need to be lost.

When she published "The Love of My Life," Strayed was a few years out from becoming Sugar, the advice columnist for *The Rumpus*, but this kind of offering would become a Sugar trademark. Strayed established not only radical empathy in this essay and in her advice columns, but radical humanism and individuality. She proclaimed that her grieving process was her own to choose. In the wake of her mother's death, "I did not deny," she writes. "I did not get angry. I didn't bargain, become depressed, or accept. I fucked. I sucked. Not my husband, but people I hardly knew, and in that I found a glimmer of relief." And along with her admissions come a critique of the way we as a culture handle and mishandle the grief of others.

> We did not always treat grief this way. Nearly every
> culture has a history, and some still have a prac-
> tice, of mourning rituals, many of which involve

changes in the dress or appearance of those in grief. The wearing of black clothing or mourning jewelry, hair cutting, and body scarification or ritual tattooing all made the grief-stricken immediately visible to the people around them. Although it is true that these practices were sometimes ridiculously restrictive and not always in the best interest of the mourner, it is also true that they gave us something of value. They imposed evidence of loss on a community and forced that community to acknowledge it. If, as a culture, we don't bear witness to grief, the burden of loss is placed entirely upon the bereaved, while the rest of us avert our eyes and wait for those in mourning to stop being sad, to let go, to move on, to cheer up. And if they don't—if they have loved too deeply, if they do wake each morning thinking, *I cannot continue to live* — well, then we pathologize their pain; we call their suffering a disease.

We do not help them: we tell them that they need to get help.

The important take-away from "The Love of My Life" and *Wild* is that self-realization is its own freedom. Perhaps Strayed reacted to her sorrow in an unconventional way. Perhaps she was "stuck" for longer than most who grieve. Forgive yourself, reader, like she did, if anyone ever told you you were having the wrong feelings and you believed them.

I suspected that these essays were the seeds that became *Wild*, so I wrote Strayed and asked her about it.

"Neither "The Love of My Life" nor "Heroin/e" are related to *Wild*," Strayed replied. "I wrote them both while I was writing my first novel, *Torch*, well before I had any inkling I'd ever write a book about my PCT hike. What happened is that by the time *Torch* was published in 2006 I had two kids under the age of two and very little time to write. Once I began thinking about what book to write after finishing with *Torch* I thought I could perhaps pull off a collection of essays, since by then I'd already written several," including the two discussed above.

She began writing an essay about the hike for the collection, and "it got longer and longer and longer and I soon saw it was actually a book. That's how *Wild* began. There are bits of both essays in the chapter about my mom's cancer and death, and obviously they cover some of the same ground, but I never thought of them as the beginning of writing *Wild*."

What then to learn from the overlap of material? There are the notable alterations when the material of the essays is transposed to the larger work of *Wild*. As with the thread of her heroin use, Strayed presents a cleaner, more removed, and more moralistic version of her behavior—this time around sex—from "The Love of My Life" to *Wild*:

> My mom had been dead a week when I kissed another man. And another a week after that. I only made out with them and the others that followed—vowing not to cross a sexual line that had some meaning to me—but I still knew I was wrong to cheat and lie.

The difference in moral judgment is stark. But this is not to say that one version of events, or one persona, is more or less authentic than the other. This is an opportunity to see how a shift in persona alters the ultimate message of the same source material.

The persona in *Wild* is someone we are confident has met resolution, whereas the persona in these two previous essays is of a person still living inside the experience of pain. The writer of *Wild* is years beyond the experience; the writer of the essays is closer, and for the first time writing the story as "truth" instead of through fiction. It follows that the language of *Wild* is more removed, while the personae in the essays use more raw descriptive language that aims its fist at the reader's gut. Strayed's essays instruct us about the bottomless possibilities of mourning, but when we open *Wild*, we have the author's unspoken promise that she will deliver us from it by the end.

Same story. Different "stories."

THEN THERE WAS THE REAL LIVE
TRULY DOING IT

At least as much as what the doing represented, *Wild* is about "the real live truly doing it." It is the story of physical endurance, a difficult hike. And I was drawn to it, like many readers, because it was the story of a woman on a difficult hike. The moral lessons of *Wild*, and of any difficult journey, are available as a direct result of the physical lessons.

When I first held it, the hardcover edition of *Wild* was a portal to nostalgia. On the book jacket: a worn brown hiking boot with silver metal fasts and frayed red laces. That boot looked an awful lot like the one I'd worn every day for eight-five days in 1992, right around the time Strayed made her own boot selection. It might have been the very same make of boot, though the laces on mine were brown and white, speckled. I studied the book cover and remembered how the inside of my right index finger was rough and calloused from tying and retying those laces: the skin was shredded and hardened and discolored. Even now, I rub my thumbs along the inside of my index fingers and feel a textural difference between the right and the left.

I like to imagine Cheryl Strayed feeling this sense of nostalgia herself when she revisited her journals and photographs and memory flashes, that her time in the wilderness had morphed into a solid piece of her history that was enjoyable, if sometimes difficult, to turn over and then recreate on the page. Writing memoir mingles the pleasant feelings of nostalgia with recollections of fear and doubt and frank suffering. The act of writing reshapes the experience and makes it about something else: the creation of a work of art, something useful to others. I often declare, joking but not really, that writing memoir is better than therapy. At the end of writing a memoir, you've created order out of your chaos, you've controlled it and made sense of it—and you've also *created something* tangible and finite, and hopefully come to understand yourself better in the process. So while in the story Cheryl suffered genuine physical pain as she lost her toenails one by one, Strayed can *marvel* over her lost toenails in retrospect, remembering the pain but no longer corporally connected to it.

The boots-on-the-ground building blocks of *Wild* are presented chronologically; but throughout the hike, Cheryl's backstory takes an equally prominent role. At the onset of her expedition, she describes the first day of walking the trail under the weight of her pack. "Which, it turns out, is not very much like walking at all. Which, in fact, resembles walking less than it does hell." This was not how she imagined it when she first considered walking the PCT. This comparison offers an opportunity for a memory trigger: situation (walking the trail) triggers story (what went wrong in her life and how she got here).

Six months prior in Minneapolis, Cheryl is eating lunch with her friend Aimee and suddenly comprehends her body's signals: she is pregnant. This pregnancy, Strayed later told *O Magazine*, was her turning point: it "was just completely symbolic of everything that I'd fucked up, and I was like, Okay, I really have to get myself out of this dark place." So mid-hell on day one on the trail, she carefully ushers us backwards in time, to this place when she first considered how the PCT might bring her back to herself. We are introduced to the man she'd been seeing, Joe, and come to understand the "troubles" she's alluded to earlier: it was Joe who introduced her to heroin, and with whom she'd made heroin a habit.

We learn about her friends' concerns about her drug use. After an abortion, Cheryl decides to buy the PCT guidebook she'd noticed while shopping with Aimee, and to "change...Not into a different person, but back to the person I used to be—strong and responsible, clear-eyed and driven, ethical and good. And the PCT would make me that way." Which delivers us back to the trail, where Cheryl confronts the real physical consequences of her decision, the hell of the hike's reality.

The braided narrative makes it easier to stay engaged with the minutia of Cheryl's hiking days. There is the clear sense on the surface narrative that the only important thing is getting through the day and getting closer to her destination of the Bridge of Gods. But "bubbling beneath" is the reader's knowledge that each successful day moves Cheryl closer to her goal of "changing." By day four, Cheryl is "having a kind of strange, abstract, retrospective fun," despite moments of terror including being charged by a Texas longhorn bull, and "all the places my skin was bleeding or blistered or red with rash—on the tips of my toes and the backs of my heels, over my hip bones and across the front of my shoulders and back." She is able to appreciate the "beauty that surrounds me, the wonder of things both small and large: the color of a desert flower that brushed against me

ALDEN JONES

on the trail or the grand sweep of sky as the sun faded over the mountains." When Cheryl identifies a lesson about solo hiking, we understand that it will become a life tool beyond the trail. After the bull charges her and then disappears, she is faced with the choice of what to do when it may return to charge her again:

> The thing about hiking the Pacific Crest Trail, the thing that was so very profound to me that summer—and yet also, like most things, so very simple—was how few choices I had and how often I had to do the thing I least wanted to do. How there was no escape or denial. No numbing it down with a martini or a roll in the hay. As I clung to the chaparral that day, attempting to patch up my bleeding finger, terrified by every sound that the bull was coming back, I considered my options. There were only two of them and they were essentially the same. I could go back in the direction I had come from, or I could go forward in the direction I intended to go. The bull, I acknowledged grimly, could be in either direction.… I could only choose between the bull that would take me back and the bull that would take me forward.
>
> And so I walked on.

Cheryl will choose this option many times over the course of *Wild*: to move forward no matter what. How many times can she conclude that she must "walk on" despite fear or pain or exhaustion or loneliness without the narrative becoming redundant? Strayed intended the chronology of her hike to be comprehensive, rather than an arrangement of only a few key scenes, so that we could feel the passage of time with her and understand the endurance involved. This put the story at high risk for the mimetic fallacy, when the narrative style mimics the content in a potentially detrimental manner: she wants us to feel her monotony and the slowness of her endurance without the narrative itself being monotonous and slow.

In addition to the braided narrative, one of the ways she skirts narrative monotony is by dovetailing the crescendo of her personal reckoning with a shift from identifying as a person who doesn't really belong on the trail, who considers herself a foreigner or a faker compared to the "real" hikers she encounters on the trail, to a full and recognized member of the PCT community. Anyone who's traveled for long stretches knows that when you first arrive in a new place you reserve more of your thoughts for the people from wherever it was you left, and regard the geography you left as your primary context; but eventually the new geography becomes the familiar context where you are simply living out your life. This is what happens to Cheryl when she finds herself in the pleasant camaraderie of other "real hikers," not as an outsider, but as one of them.

Cheryl wanted to become a seasoned and capable hiker, so she behaves like one until she is one. When she begins viewing herself as just another hiker on the trail, sharing goals and stories and food and goodwill with her fellow hikers, the narrative acquires a new texture, and is populated by characters occupying her present space as much as the memories of those at home. It contains more brightness. Things get easier, both physically and psychically. Cheryl has embodied the maxim, popular on Outward Bound, of "fake it 'til you make it."

What Cheryl had done for herself was one of the prime Outward Bound lessons. An entire school, and many like it, was built around the goals she set for herself and accomplished. Self-reliance was not something someone else could do for you. You earned it by performing it.

BOOTS ON THE GROUND

Outward Bound was founded by Kurt Hahn, whose educational philosophy was rooted in the idea that "The aim of education is to impel people into value-forming experiences, to ensure the survival of these qualities:

an enterprising curiosity,
an indefatigable spirit,
tenacity in pursuit,
readiness for sensible self-denial,
and above all, compassion."

I was one of twelve in the crew. We were seven women and five men inches beyond being girls and boys. We existed under the guidance, education, and ultimately the policing of 26-year-old Eliot, a wiry outdoorsman with boundless energy, and 40-year-old Robin, a semi-closeted lesbian with chronic back pain and cheeks deeply scarred from a motorcycle accident. I grew close to Robin in the end, but for the first weeks we resented the pair of them with great passion. As a group, we had spirit and tenacity. But a readiness for self-denial and above all, compassion? In those departments we were short.

Eliot and Robin believed in a hard Outward Bound line. We did things the most difficult way they could be done or we received a lecture about "challenging ourselves." They offered the briefest lessons in orienteering, then sat back and watched as we turned the map the wrong way, missed geographical cues, and stalked off course. They confiscated Thermarest sleeping pads and rock climbing shoes, asserting there were no shortcuts or special comforts. Some Outward Bound leaders allowed coffee or black tea, but to our leaders, caffeine was a crutch.

Aside from two breaks, one at the end of each month, we did not stop running, hiking, climbing, paddling, preparing meals, organizing gear, scrubbing pots, setting up camp, and breaking down camp for three months. We were hairy and filthy and scabbed and scarred. When I arrived at the AT, I did not know how to pitch a tent, tie a proper knot, light a camping stove, attach a harness for climbing, or wring out my clothes so they actually had a chance of drying before we broke down camp. When I didn't know how to execute a task, I turned to look for a helpful boy, and in this way it took me longer than it should have to learn how to tie a proper knot or set up the sleeping tarp.

When it was time to switch out our gear and obtain our food resupply we spent the day at the Outward Bound base camp. The thing we loved more than anything about base camp was the bathroom. In the indoor bathroom three toilets sat in a row, no doors or dividers between them, facing a row of sinks. Sinks, WITH SOAP. Once I found a bottle of Pert Plus tucked into the corner of the bathroom and secretly washed my hair in the sink. All afternoon my crew mates grilled me, "Why do you smell so good? Why do you look so good?" I shrugged as they eyed me suspiciously, their hair greasy and matted. As we relieved ourselves in the basecamp bathroom, so insanely grateful for porcelain and plumbing, we continued whatever conversations we'd been having prior to pulling down our pants. When you were used to being physically at your limit at all times, shame went out the window.

We had no shame. We cried, swore, kicked trees. We argued over routes, pace, divvying up gear, and especially food. We ate things that packed easily into our seventy-pound backpacks, things that didn't spoil: powdered hummus and falafel; grocery store bagels; peanut butter and jelly rationed in plastic bags that we punctured and squeezed; "Chunks O' Chicken" in generically labeled cans. I remember the food in great detail because we were always hungry.

It rained almost constantly on the North Carolina section of the Appalachian Trail in September of 1992. We ate our lunch of cheese and crackers while rivulets of rainwater snaked down our hoods and into our polypropylene undershirts. I would have killed for a dry, clean pair of socks. We climbed rock, canoed, rappelled, caved. We acquired skills. We told jokes and posed riddles. We sang every song we knew from start to finish. We flirted with each other because it was our greatest pleasure; actual intimacy was strictly verboten: It compromised self-reliance. But we would learn how to get around those rules.

On our feet, astounding blisters; pinky toes transitioned into tiny, whitened nubs. We had "Circle Time" during which we processed our experiences, our group dynamic, and discussed how to—we groaned in anticipation of the phrase—"challenge ourselves." We traveled from the Appalachian Trail in North Carolina to the Everglades in Florida, where the mosquitoes were so bad we used 100% DEET to fend them off. If we leaned a DEET-sprayed leg against a plastic backpack liner, or slid cheap sunglasses onto a DEET-slathered face, the plastic melted, leaving black smears on our skin. We spent three days in canoes without stepping on land. Whoever drew the shortest straws had to sleep on the edges of the lashed-together canoes, their bodies as still and stiff as the boards underneath us so as not to roll into the black water. (It seemed a miracle no one rolled into the water.) We canoed all the way to the Gulf of Mexico, and slept each night on a different deserted island. Had we gotten along better, and minus the mosquitoes, it might have been paradise.

The trip culminated in the climb of the 17,400-foot dormant volcano Iztaccíhuatl, 43 miles northwest of Mexico City. Full ascent took us a week. Three of the group developed altitude sickness, and a fourth—our consummately fit leader, Eliot—was hospitalized, his lungs perforated. The summit was above the clouds. I'd never seen anything like it: Look down, and below you, a carpet of clouds. It suggested it would hold you if you jumped. We hiked narrow ridges in the snow, wearing spiked shoe attachments called crampons. For days I was nauseated and short of breath, but I kept swallowing food, and I kept ascending, because by now I understood that it was possible to override the protests of my body. The angle was steep, and we tied into ropes to traverse dangerous crevasses, rappelling each other as the wind ripped at our cheeks. It was easy to imagine falling to our deaths. Over twenty years later, it remains recorded in my muscles, how to wield an ice axe in order to halt a fall down a snowy mountainside. Our feet were so cold in our boots, the only way to warm them up was to take off our boots, and then our socks, and place our bare feet on the belly of a friend.

With one or two exceptions, we had all chosen this hard line Outward Bound expedition because there was something we were struggling with. To a person, we were there to become better than we were—physically, but mostly otherwise.

The physical effort and strain I faced were significant. When I returned home and finally saw myself in a full-length mirror, I did not recognize my own muscular legs. But the most difficult thing about this Outward Bound course was that there was no escape from each other. No option, when tension got thick, of uttering, "fuck you people! I'm going home," and going home, or anywhere else. Even if we wanted to go off and be alone further in the woods Outward Bound's safety rules prohibited separation. Everyone knew where everyone else was at all times. We were stuck, in the wilderness, with each other.

No books to escape into. They were too heavy. And Outward Bound discouraged books. The idea was, we faced each moment, we confronted our problems; escape was the enemy. I wrote over two hundred pages in my journal, but I didn't read. We talked. We knew each other. We saw each other at our strongest, but more often, we saw each other at our weakest.

There were face-offs, freeze-outs, tense disagreements. During one expedition, our leaders instructed us to hike off trail. Off trail, every step meant skin scratched by brambles, and without a path to follow we would have to navigate every ten feet. We would get lost. We were always lost. "Why are we doing this? There is a *trail*," Ellen said. "Isn't the whole fucking point of hiking the Appalachian Trail to FOLLOW THE TRAIL?" Others got angry with our leaders' directive and pushed back. Our leaders offered no explanation. "Accept the challenge," they said, their frustration with us only fueling our disapproval of everything they asked. When we accepted they wouldn't budge and lifted each other's packs to leave the comfort of the pounded dirt and step into the brush, we realized that Ellen had disappeared. We found her way off trail, sitting on her pack, refusing to move. "Go on without me," Ellen said in an eerie monotone. "I'll hitchhike to Atlanta. The road isn't far. I know people in Atlanta. I don't want to hold you back. Go ahead. I'll be fine." There were many episodes like that one. Even during these moments, there was the dense cloud of love that surrounds people who have endured something together.

The things I struggled with at home followed me to the trail. I struggled with the fact of being female, the "weaker sex." I struggled with being slow. I struggled with how often I requested help from boys—at first. I struggled with my attraction to boys.

I struggled when I baited strait-laced crew mates I'd just met, testing their comfort with ideas about queerness, and confirmed their homophobia. I struggled with being a person who baited. I struggled with how much I enjoyed using my feminine wiles, how naturally it came to me, how hard it was going to be to give it up. Because I was going to have to give it up. I struggled, but in a more exciting way, with my attraction to a girl. Melissa with the black boots. Melissa was not here to make friends, and that was delightful about her. She didn't care if we liked her or not. She was here to "challenge herself," and took every challenge she was offered with guts and grit.

Above all, Melissa had compassion. Something I needed. I needed to embody it. But I didn't know how to embody compassion yet. So I started to consider how I might raid hers.

Of course, I didn't see it that way at the time.

I thought it was about getting my body and her body into some impossibly private geography. I still believed the thing I was after had to do with bodies.

A NOTE ON THE CONSTRUCTION
OF THIS BOOK

The section you have just finished reading is the first section I wrote when I began *The Wanting Was a Wilderness*. I added the last three paragraphs later and tweaked sentences here and there, but otherwise it remains here exactly as I first wrote it.

I thought this section would commence my memoir portion of this book. But after I wrote it I still couldn't locate the center of the story. I put this section aside. I reread *Wild* and started at a new beginning, with the idea of Maps.

By the time I wrote through to this section, my story was starting to push its way out of the dirt. Of course it was about Melissa. But it was also not about Melissa at all. It was what I learned about myself in my proximity to not only Melissa, but the forces of energy around us—the antagonists I would only be able to identify by continuing to write.

Back I go to set it up. I write "My Own System(at)ic Oppression," position it into an early part of the story. Then I read through to this section again, looking for edges to spackle and spade. I write myself back to this spot.

This section does the job of giving you the big picture of my story, the boots-on-the-ground plot. Now I can slow down and hone in on the moments that offer some narrative payoff.

A narrative needs conflict; my situation has no shortage there. But which of these conflicts merit the focus that will best offer up my message or "story"? There was Melissa, of course, whom I now need to present as a more complete character. But there was also the way I was changing because of the physical challenges I faced while isolated from the rest of the world.

Somehow, these stories must collide.

THE CREW

Within a day our crew split gently into two social groups. I found myself in the group that contained the big personalities, the extroverts, those with the greater sense of entitlement, and the social leaders, who began flirting with each other immediately. I found myself directing attention towards a kind-seeming boy, John with the eyelashes and blue eyes. John allied with Brandon, a quiet but similarly tall and handsome boy who visually belonged next to him. Ellen and I became a unified front of skirting unpleasant duties and saving each other the best spots in the middle of the tarp. She was hilariously funny and made up songs on the trail that stuck with us for entire expeditions. Along with Ellen, Andrea was also an instant friend. She was pretty and preternaturally cheerful and great in the kitchen. Peter was our rock, good-natured and physically by far the strongest, eager to help when his strength was required. He made me laugh constantly. The other group formed by default. They were the introverts, the loners, the ones who seemed to be in true emotional turmoil, a quiet girl named Caitlin who would emerge at the end of the 85 days one of my closest friends, a guitar-playing boy named Jake who was quick to anger, and Melissa.

Melissa, from Indiana, had spent a year at Evergreen College in Olympia, Washington, which I'd heard made Brown look Republican, but she wasn't going back. She had just come off following the Grateful Dead with her sister and, for the final two weeks, a boy named Edward she'd fallen in love with at one of the shows. After spending those two weeks with Edward she'd decided to make a life with him. (My private assessment upon learning this: *questionable relationship judgment.*) They planned to meet up a few months after Outward Bound and travel together in Central America. Melissa knew all about camping and outdoor cooking and sleeping outside and spending days on end unshowered. She was quick to volunteer for tasks, and, though she was the smallest member of the crew, she always carried more weight than anyone else.

When I watched Melissa effortlessly stake a tarp while I fumbled with the metal bars, I felt a combination of alienation, envy, and admiration. Obviously we could not be friends. Her social life around the Grateful Dead was enough to thwart that possibility. A friend had pressed me to listen to their music once, and I'd sincerely given it a chance, but concluded that nothing about the music, the social milieu, or the aesthetic offered even the tiniest draw. It wasn't a value judgment. I preferred synth-pop and club music in the vein of Deee-Lite, and was aware that didn't place me in any category of superior taste. I just perceived no entrance into that crowd. When I pictured myself at a Dead show, I was sober, arms crossed, grossly out of place in my platform clogs and dark lipstick, grimacing with confusion at all the tripping, swirling kids with their easy smiles. *Too easy.*

But maybe that was the problem. People like Melissa knew how to be happy in a simple way and I didn't have it in me. Everything that made me happy involved intensity. I felt most joyful when I was in love, on a dark dance floor, traveling somewhere unfamiliar, having immersive conversations in an academic context, singing in rehearsal/performance settings, and deep into a difficult book. Once Melissa called me over, saying, "I want you to hear something." She'd heard a dog barking in the distance. "Listen to the echo the barking is making," she said, blissed out by this simple sound and wanting me to share it with her. Why couldn't I appreciate life in this way, I wondered, straining to enjoy the sound of the echo while my mind spun a wild and messy narrative about my inability to enjoy the simple things in life.

Melissa's wilderness know-how and gutsy attitude also pushed my ignorance and incapability into relief. I didn't want to spend too much time near that. But at the same time, I wanted some of what she had.

I wouldn't be friends with Melissa.

But what would it be like to *be like* Melissa?

It didn't take long for Peter and me to establish a routine of sleeping next to each other under the tarp, him opening his arm for me to snuggle into, breathing in each other's faces as we fell asleep. Though we would never have discovered each other in the real world, I adored Peter and I enjoyed his attention. I fell in with the extroverts because they were fun.

But they were also attached to the world I'd started to leave behind. They made, and laughed at, wife-beating jokes; they uttered "what a faggot" as if it were punctuation. I responded with stories of New York, of social and sexual deviance. I was deliberately trying to alienate them, yet felt hurt when some of them started pulling away from me when I did.

Naturally, there was no way to discuss my theoretical preoccupations in this non-academic setting without coming across as an asshole. Almost half the crew arrived at Outward Bound after dropping out of college and were struggling with what to do next. Any discussion involving my academic and feminist fixations did nothing but alienate them further. Years later, I would become an educator concerned with presenting difficult ideas in a way those new to them could understand, but I was nowhere near possessing the level of empathy I'd need to perform this job. Just as some of my classmates and professors had made me feel inferior for not *a priori* knowing things, I did to my Outward Bound crew mates. Once, in response to something I'd said, Andrea innocently asked "What's misogyny?" and instead of answering her question, I looked at her with shocked disapproval. I knew how to shut people down, but I didn't yet know how to lift them up. I could include a sentence now designed to let me off the hook, linking this instinct to my insecurity, and it would be true. But also true: sometimes I was just an asshole.

John, at first, always arrived at my side to help me when it was my turn to set up the tarp. But when I told a story about a party at Tavern on the Green I'd gone to over the summer with my friend Margaret—we made it past the velvet rope, and there was Lady Miss Kier of Deee-Lite, surrounded by the most glamorous drag queens!—and that led to a story of me dressing up my friend David in my clothes and makeup for an LGBA dance, both John and Brandon stared at me like I was an unfamiliar creature, something alien and untrustworthy. John was slower to return my smiles after that. After I was outed during a dry game of I Never as someone who'd "kissed, or messed around, or anything with someone of the same sex," John frankly avoided me.

I could not have it both ways. The day after I Never, I wrote in my journal: "I let too much hang out last night." Then I wrote: "I feel trapped." What did I want? To be considered likeable by everyone, or to be free? I didn't want to have to choose. But I would have to choose.

Melissa, throughout this, was unflappable. An unflappable hippie who believed in love and acceptance and honesty and kindness. She neither blinked at Ellen when she said "what a faggot" nor at me when stories of "my gay friends" inched closer what I really wanted to say. She did not tell people how to be. I kept my eye on Melissa as I zigzagged through the highs and lows of the first month, the ease with which she used her body and the comfort she had with her body, and the suspicion that she was probably the only person in the immense expanse of forest I now inhabited that I could be truthful with.

Our final expedition of Month One was disastrous. Robin and Eliot must have used a secret satellite phone to call Base Camp and tell them we had strayed off course and would arrive days late. It rained and rained and rained. Our rain gear began to emit a foul smell that Robin likened to cat pee. We began rationing food and flashlight batteries and hoarding strike-anywhere matches. The mood plummeted.

Rest periods shrank so they were just long enough to chew food and chug water. Even Melissa's face went sour. A rift formed between the boys, who would have been more than happy to sacrifice the slower members of the group in order to finish the expedition, and the girls, who were tired of being barked at to pick up the pace as if we weren't at our limit. John glared and snapped at everyone except Andrea and Brandon. Ellen exclaimed "everybody smells like ass!" Caitlin muttered under her breath. Jake assumed Caitlin was muttering about him and exploded on her in rage. Caitlin cried. I made vaguely accusatory statements about the abuse of male power. Peter and I did not even consider cuddling.

Ahead of us on the trail, someone yelled "BEES!" Brandon turned around and waited for me to run the other way, but I was too tired so I just stood there and looked and him, like, *yeah?* I could handle bee stings; I could not handle running. Brandon was terrified of bees, as if we all hadn't been stung twenty or thirty times by now. "What are you doing? They said BEES!" He shoved me aside, hard, leaving me suspended in the rhododendrons. I sagged into the mesh of branches and cried. Andrea and Caitlin brought me an orange and pulled me upright by my pack straps, coaxing me back onto the trail.

"I'm so weak," I moaned. I moaned a lot about being weak. It was kind of my thing during Month One. I moaned about the unfairness of biology. When would the world bend around my idea of fairness? I would stay mad until it did. I complained, complained.

Was the wilderness beautiful? Was the AT majestic and inspiring? It probably was, but most of the time our eyes were on our boots on the dirt, the pack moving in front of us. When we summited a peak with an expansive view of the mountains, we huffed and paused, muttered "pretty," and walked on.

The military issue maps, our leaders finally revealed to us, were fifty years old. A spot that marked an orchard—a crosshatched section of white and green we'd never encountered on the map before—was assumed to be some kind of semi-clearing. But the orchard had since overgrown, and now presented as regular uncleared forest. Navigating without this information, we wound up on a peak way above where we needed to be. We broke for snack and then packed up to set off in the wrong direction when Eliot and Robin finally relented.

"We are actually only a few hundred feet from our destination," Eliot said. "It's right down there."

Eliot decoded the map for us. He pointed down a slick, unwalkable slope overgrown with poison ivy. No discussion was required: we abandoned the trail, sat down on our packs and began sliding down the slope. We arrived at the end point with ripped and filthy clothes, covered in scratches and plastered with dirt. Poison ivy rashes blossomed on our arms and legs the next day. But we were done.

We did not feel triumphant. We had achieved the physical goal. But the lessons we were supposed to internalize were absent in the wake of the bickering and blame and aggravation. I felt no closer to self-reliance or self-understanding, and now my relationships in the crew were fraught, some of them maybe even broken.

As I dipped my dirt-smeared clothes into the river, I recognized with utter clarity that frustration, the dominant emotion of the moment, was not what I came here for. Something was going to have to shift. And I would have to be the person who shifted it.

I also knew that I had accomplished physical feats that I had never attempted before. I *was* stronger than I'd known. The metaphor had not reached its full development—I still didn't see how meeting physical challenges made me a better person or more psychologically calm or together. But two months in the wilderness remained. I acknowledged possibility.

Downriver, Melissa squatted in the shallows, naked in defiance of Outward Bound rules. Melissa disdained the "no nudity" guideline. It was the only rule she broke. (So far.) She bent forward and rinsed out her hair. She didn't seem to mind that the water was cold. She didn't care if someone might see her. Maybe she even knew I was there. I watched her with great interest. I stripped down to my sports bra and my ex-boyfriend's lacrosse shorts. I entered the stream.

At the end of Month One we broke for three days. I flew home to New Jersey and hung out with my mom and ate all of my favorite foods and soaked in a very clean bathtub for a very long time. I called friends and got caught up on their normal lives. I flew back to North Carolina. When I arrived at base camp, I walked directly to the spot where Melissa was tending the trail. It was our responsibility to leave the trail and camp better than we found it. I reached for a shovel.

"Hi," I said, and dug with her.

I told Melissa about H. About the other girls. I told her everything. She talked about her love for Edward. She said no one left Evergreen straight. She'd thought about women, too, abstractly. We talked for an hour. She told me I was stronger than I gave myself credit for. I believed her. Month Two was going to be a different kind of month.

Melissa unrolled her sleeping bag next to mine that night. When I woke in the morning light I found her staring at me. "I had a dream about you," she said. The nerve switch silently flipped. Now it was just a matter of when.

THE URGE TO REVISE THE PAST

I grappled with that last bit. The paragraph about being an asshole—I wrote it, took it out, put it back in, fine-tuned it, and left it. Do I really need to admit that I condescended to my crew mates, my friends, in this way? Yet I know it is important to admit that I did, even if I see it as misguided and shameful now. And if any of my crew mates are reading this, they are probably glad I included this information, because it was a true, and I'm sure a defining, aspect of their experience with me.

At the same time that I am making these considerations with my own persona, hoping I will not alienate the reader (though one of the "messages" of this book, I hope, is that if you try to please everyone you will never be free—I peacefully accept that not everyone will like me, and this is precisely what allows me to be free), I am using some caution out of respect for the people in this story. They are real people. When *Unaccompanied*

ALDEN JONES

Minors came out, a few of my crew mates read it; a flurry of photos from our trip popped up on social media around the book's publication. They, too, have evolved into more self-realized people. The people who uttered homophobic slurs then posted rainbow flag profile pictures in support of same-sex marriage legalization twenty years later. If they are reading this, they are probably surprised to remember the degree of their disgust around queerness. They might even want to deny it because they can no longer remember feeling that way. (Apologies, friends; I wrote it all down.) Cultural norms have shifted drastically, and human beings have a psychological tendency to revise the histories of our belief systems to adhere to what's acceptable now.

Indeed, I did not remember the degree of my own internalized homophobia until I re-read my Outward Bound journal. I remembered myself as more radical than I was. I remembered making out with Peter practically nightly that first month, when my journal revealed I only made out with him twice; more often, we ran our hands over each other's bodies as silently as we could. I remembered Melissa as more confident in the world than she was, until I re-read the letter tucked into my Outward Bound journal that she'd slipped me to read on the plane home. She was a lost kid, trying to find

THE WANTING WAS A WILDERNESS

direction. I remember her as impossibly free-spirited, a nomad of the highest order. My Outward Bound journal is written by a girl wracked with self-doubt and worry. Melissa saw me as clear-eyed and directed. I remembered her as powerful over me. Her letter revealed how much power she felt I'd had over her.

"I am also attracted to the confusion, the uncertainty, that I see inside you," Melissa wrote. "Maybe this is because I have so much inside me." How negotiable our wilderness looks in retrospect. How easy it seems to machete-cut an exit path.

I would love to reconstruct my character to be wiser, more together, less of a complainer, always charitable, badass and radical instead of filled with self-doubt and a fear of being disliked. And this is why it was so much easier to write this story as fiction when I was still embarrassed of these qualities that defined my younger self. It is easier to mock one's youthful concerns than it is to have sympathy for them. Insulting someone is the ultimate act, the basic schoolyard instinct, of Othering: *I am not that.* In order write a true story, you must be unrelentingly sympathetic towards the person you truly were at the time of the events. The fallibility of memory makes this difficult, but the effort must be there. (Diaries help. Conversations with people who were there help.) If you impose the belief system and the knowledge you have now on the person you were many years ago, you are not writing a true story at all.

In order to render sympathy for that person, you must hold them accountable, and you must also forgive them.

We might call this the Sugar approach.

ACCOUNTABILITY IN THE
REDEMPTION MEMOIR

The idea of holding a person—oneself or someone else—accountable for their actions is precisely what renders Strayed's brand of empathy "radical." Sympathy alone is not enough. Consider the friends or loved ones in your life (we all have one) who have a way of making questionable decisions and then finding themselves in emotional, financial, or physical peril as a result, and who then require help. What happens when you offer only empathy, sharing the emotional toll of their trauma and validating their feelings without helping them understand how their choices might have yielded the results? They will likely repeat their actions. And if you only offer tough love, chastising them for their behavior, you are not providing any emotional support for any real trauma they face, which is cruel, and also creates a disconnect between you and that person.

For a reckoning to occur, a delicate balance between sympathy and accountability is requisite.

This is also true of writing oneself as a character in memoir. Countless lesser memoirs position the author/persona as someone deserving of great sympathy, but who rarely does anything you might judge negatively (unless they can blame it on the villain of the story). James Frey took victim status to a new level in *A Million Little Pieces*, the 2003 "memoir" that was ultimately exposed as nonfiction fraud, when he wrote in fictional scenes that solicited extravagant sympathy from the reader: depicting a classmate's tragic death as the loss of the only person who ever understood him (a girl in his high school died as he described, but her parents were bewildered that Frey painted himself as her dearest friend, as they had never heard his name); detailing a callous and harrowing dental experience supposedly sanctioned by professionals at Hazelton (I read it and thought, "how crazy, that a renowned rehab center would greet a new patient by performing a root canal with no anesthetic... but it's a memoir, so I guess it happened"). After *The Smoking Gun* exposed these and other false claims, Random House asked him to write a preface for subsequent editions of *A Million Little Pieces* explaining his actions. In it, Frey owned up to the more blatant fictions,

THE WANTING WAS A WILDERNESS

then made an interesting statement about wanting to
appear a certain way to others—and to himself:

> I made other alterations in my portrayal of myself,
> most of which portrayed me in ways that made
> me tougher and more daring and more aggressive
> than in reality I was, or I am. People cope with
> adversity in many different ways, ways that are
> deeply personal. I think one way people cope is
> by developing a skewed perception of themselves
> that allows them to overcome and do things they
> thought they couldn't do before. My mistake, and
> it is one I deeply regret, is writing about the person
> I created in my mind to help me cope, and not the
> person who went through the experience.

This is an extreme version of a common "trauma
memoir" miscalculation, and also a cautionary tale for
memoirists at risk for manipulating not only the truth, but
the reader. Certainly, memory is fallible, and facts will be
altered innocently. Sometimes unintentional self-revision
is the result of a lack of self-examination. Self-examination
is not possible without accountability—a hard look at
one's past self. This is something all memoirists should
require of themselves. Without it you risk pillaging the
reader's trust.

A frequent comparison to *Wild* is Elizabeth Gilbert's *Eat, Pray, Love* (2006). Elizabeth Gilbert is a skilled writer, and I don't wish to diminish the profound impact *Eat, Pray, Love* had on the personal-essay travel writing genre; however, there is a keen difference between *Wild* and *Eat, Pray, Love* on the level of self-examination. Both memoirs were runaway hits that reached a wide readership (primarily female), and both are held up as inspirational stories of redemption after a period of "falling apart." But in *Eat, Pray, Love*, Gilbert tiptoes around the forces that led her to crying on the bath-room floor, quickly painting the backstory of a vaguely unhappy marriage, focusing instead on her journey back to herself, rather than what, precisely, required redemption in the first place. The "in" for the reader of *Eat, Pray, Love* is precisely this vagueness: the reader is invited to fill in this blank with whatever might have caused them to fall apart, and offers one example of how to emerge from it (travel).

In 2015, nine years after *Eat, Pray, Love*'s publication, Gilbert wrote the short personal essay "Confessions of a Seduction Addict" for the *New York Times*, revealing that she had omitted quite a bit of information about her psychological state, the end of her first marriage, and her compulsive behavior during and before the time of events in *Eat, Pray, Love*:

> You might have called me a serial monogamist, except that I was never exactly monogamous. Relationships overlapped, and those overlaps were always marked by exhausting theatricality: sobbing arguments, shaming confrontations, broken hearts. Still, I kept doing it. I couldn't not do it.… I would plan the heist for months, scouting out the target, looking for unguarded entries. Then I would break into his deepest vault, steal all his emotional currency and spend it on myself.

In "Confessions of a Seduction Addict" Gilbert comes clean about the heart of her earlier emotional turmoil, "confesses" to the turmoil she caused others, and performs the reckoning that is absent from *Eat, Pray, Love*. "I forced myself to admit that I had a problem—indeed, that I was a problem. Tinkering with other people's most vulnerable emotions didn't make me a romantic; it just made me a swindler. Lying and cheating didn't make me brazen; it just made me a needy coward. Stealing other women's boyfriends didn't make me a revolutionary feminist; it just made me a menace. I hated that it took me almost 20 years to realize this."

Self-examination arrived in a neatly packaged essay many years later. I dare say it would only have enriched *Eat, Pray, Love* if she had included and unpacked this part of her history, and now that we have this knowledge, it forces the reader to consider what else might have been glossed over in *Eat, Pray, Love*. But perhaps, at the time of the writing, Gilbert had not yet reached an understanding of her accountability. Or perhaps a reader or an editor expressed concern that if she came clean about her recklessness with others, a reader's ability to connect with her would be compromised.

Memoirs that focus on redemption alone that do hold up are usually those of extreme situations where survival is at stake. Certainly there are nonfiction accounts in which accountability is a non-issue, in which the persona is an unqualified victim of evil forces and/or terrible people: slavery and holocaust narratives and other first-person accounts of large-scale persecution; family-focused memoirs in which simply emerging from childhood able to write a book is a triumph, such as Jeanette Walls's *The Glass Castle*, Tara Westover's *Educated*, Jerald Walker's *The World in Flames*, and Frank McCourt's *Angela's Ashes*. In the case of these memoirs, self-analysis or any commentary from the present-day author "who knows how it all worked out" is rarely needed. When Jeanette Walls describes her dress catching on fire as she is cooking hot dogs for herself at three years old, recovering from serious burns in the hospital, and her parents' insanely flip reaction to all of this, she does not need to qualify the danger she was in. It is hard to argue that she had responsibility for any of her choices in the context of her poverty and familial instability. This variety of redemption memoir is cleaner. But it is not readily at hand to those of us working with less morally clear-cut material, with less available villains.

Creators of nonfiction are duty-bound to resist the urge to simplify value judgments, including being willing to position themselves as morally complex, if they hope to tell a true story rather than simply entertain or pontificate. At the same time, memoirists have leeway to smooth out facts if doing so retains the spirit of the truth: restructuring timelines; creating composite characters; recreating dialogue that can't be recalled word-for-word. The border between "truth" and "fiction" is a razor-fine line for journalists, who, by the rules of the genre, can only claim what can be proven by evidence. For memoirists, the line of demarcation is fuzzier and far more capacious, and each memoirist must decide the breadth of their own "spirit of the truth."

Claiming, as James Frey did, that you spent 87 days in jail when it was actually only a few hours, is empirically not in the "spirit of the truth." Might you fudge one day in jail to two or three, if the narrative called for it? Some memoirists would say yes, others no. We can credit James Frey and his *A Million Little Pieces* subterfuge for raising awareness of the unspoken contract between the writer and the reader of memoir regarding parameters of truthfulness, and for prompting a more considered discussion of ethics among a larger number of writers and readers. (Just after Frey was outed, my sister asked me "What do you think about the *Million Little Pieces* fiasco?" And I replied, "I'm just so happy this many people are getting worked up about a *book*!")

There are the facts memoirists alter for innocent reasons or for structural reasons. There are also facts memoirists fudge in order to be seen as a certain kind of person. A likeable one. "There is a certain impulse in all writers to want to please," Dorothy Allison told *Garden & Gun* in 2019. "You have to give up wanting to please." But as human beings concerned with enduring in our communities, this is neither a natural nor social-ized instinct.

In "On Likability," Lacy M. Johnson suggests to nonfiction writers that

The pressure to be likable...keeps us from telling the truth.... We feel pressure to disfigure ourselves on the page in these same ways [we do in life]— we constrict our stories because we are told they do not deserve to occupy space in the world, we tidy up our histories to make them more present-able to others, we carve up lifetimes of mistakes and wrong choices until the story we tell is only a shell of the truth, which isn't really any kind of truth at all...

You should be a little afraid of the story you are telling, too. And if you're not afraid that someone won't like it you're still not telling the truth.

Is telling the truth really so much more important than being likable? It is, if you want to be free—free to self-express without shame or a fear of being found out. "I think," Johnson writes, "perhaps, one reason— maybe the primary reason—that the world tries so hard to pressure us to be likable (and to punish us when we aren't) is because they are afraid we will realize that if we don't need anyone to like us we can be any way we want. We can tell any story." What incredible possibil-ities for selfhood accompany resisting the forces telling us to turn against ourselves.

Wild is, on one level, a "trauma memoir" in keeping with Sven Birkerts's description: "trauma-based narratives are crisis-centered. The pain that leads to breakage is not only intense, it is very often situation-based. Something happened—something explosive. The narrator's assumptions about the world were shattered, bringing about collapse or some other severe reaction. Eventually—and the memoir itself, the writing of it, is testament to this—some understanding or acceptance was achieved." Within this framework, a safer "shell" narrative was available to Strayed that might have focused on the unfairness of her mother's death, the shattering of her remaining family, and how lost she felt; the hike alone might have served as her path to "understanding or acceptance." There is enough story arc here, and this plot might have yielded a fine book. That Strayed chose to dive deeply into the details of her complex reaction to the death, took herself to task, and realized the importance of her own accountability as a human in the world—that she wagered likability in order to arrive at a truer truth—is the key both to her redemption and to what elevates this book to "inspirational" status. *Wild* is not essentially about getting over a death. It is about self-fulfillment on a basic human level, the result of Strayed's reckoning not about her mother's death, but about who she, Cheryl Strayed, wanted to be in the world.

Atlantic writer Elizabeth Greenwood made an interesting distinction between *Wild* and *Eat, Pray, Love*: "*Eat, Pray, Love*'s undertone is that you deserve to be happy; *Wild*'s is that you have to earn it." Gilbert's message, she says, is an indulgent one—"indulge your appetites; find enlightenment"—whereas Strayed's method of "hauling her needed possessions on her back down a free trail...or her gospel of 'nobody is going to give you a thing'" is one of accountability. The person who turns to external (and in Gilbert's case, expensive) sources for help and enlightenment is lucky when she finds them; the average reader can only fantasize that she might travel the world eating delicious food in Italy and retreating to an ashram in India and ultimately finding love in Bali. The person who seeks help and enlightenment only from herself and finds them has figured out how to live when fortune does *not* favor her. Most readers can access a journey that involves committing to a personal physical challenge. Strayed's story asks us not to fantasize about how our lives could change; it asks us consider our own accountability to enact the change we need in our lives.

FAKE IT 'TIL YOU MAKE IT

I'd looked to external forces, to the institution of a wilderness education program, for enlightenment, and while I now understood how much weight I could carry and how far I could hike, I was no closer to any kind of inner conviction. My leaders, particularly Robin, had been encouraging me to turn inward all month. But I couldn't do it until I could.

Early in Month Two we boarded a van to Tennessee for a three-night caving expedition. Our crew had spent a full morning emptying our packs, organizing gear at basecamp, and redistributing the group gear. But when we met our expedition leader after a long van ride across the border from North Carolina, we realized we had arrived to spend four days in an expansive series of caves and no one had packed a single cooking pot.

Instantly our crew dissolved into finger-pointing and gloom. Who was the jackass who was supposed to pack the pots? The expedition was doomed. Lon, our expedition leader whom we'd met at the mouth of the cave, looked at us with the surprise that let us know must groups didn't act like this.

"Of course you can go on. What's the problem?" Lon asked.

We didn't get along, we explained. Our last expedition had been a disaster, we told him. It turned out Lon was not the "circle up" variety of OB leader. He didn't want to hear about our feelings.

"None of that 'getting along' stuff matters," Lon said. "Just decide you are going to get along. Have you ever heard 'fake it 'til you make it'? Whatever you want to be, decide that you are that thing. Then do it. Now, let's troubleshoot the cooking pot situation."

We tossed around ideas for how to cook for three nights without pots inside the caves. We landed on replacing the pots with our metal mixing bowls. Dinner preparation in the caves would be slow. We usually cooked with three pots while using two bowls for the food items we stirred and chopped. But each time we drew cooking crew and cooked dinner in the bowls, I felt a quiet cloud of pride settle over the group. We fed ourselves and each other. We went on.

Inside the caves existed a different planet than the one I'd known. Outward Bound outfitted us in military uniforms so antique they included headlamps we filled with combustible material and then lit with a match. The only source of light came from the fire on our helmets. Tiny bats hibernated, clinging to the cavesides by their toenails. I leaned in close to one, observing it in awe, a little black mouse with wings, until Melissa reminded me I might singe it if I got too close, or at least bump it out of hibernation with the heat of my flame.

As for my attraction to Melissa, I set that flame to low. There was no room in the close air of the mud-walled caves for that energy. But when the last Petzl twisted off and we lay clustered together in the black dark, I quietly and invisibly tended that flame and its steady burn until sleep came.

There was a lot to awe over inside those caves. Huge "rooms" were stacked with stalactites and stalagmites and the ceiling of one cavernous room appeared splattered with glitter. In the pitch black, we sat in a circle and bit into wintergreen Life Savers Lon distributed with our front teeth, watching sparks fly around each other's lips. We never knew what time it was (watches had been confiscated), and followed the schedule Lon set for us. At the end of the expedition, Lon told us we'd only slept four hours a night in order to make better time. "And you didn't even feel tired, did you? You worked all day after four hours of sleep for three days and with no complaining. So now you know you can do it again."

This was the primary mission of Outward Bound: to learn how to do something the hardest way possible, so the next time it would be easier. So you knew you *could* do it. More skills-based programs taught rock climbing with expert-level harnesses and climbing shoes. On Outward Bound we learned rock climbing by knotting a stretch of seatbelt webbing into an awkward but functional harness, then ascending walls of rock in bulky sneakers, slipping often, getting really good at falling before we were good at climbing. Skills were important, but they were secondary to determination in the face of setback.

Three days before the caving expedition I'd tripped and fallen on a gravel road during a morning run. As Andrea and I jogged along a downhill slope of road, I noticed a protruding rock that I assumed was a large hunk of gravel, and kept my pace rather than avoiding it. But the rock wasn't kicked out of my path by my sneaker; it caught me, and my arms flew out in front of me, and I skidded downhill on my belly, sliding to a stop ten or fifteen feet from where I'd fallen, both elbows and both knees unconditionally skinned.

Andrea knelt down next to me. "You stole home base!" she said. "That was incredible!" Andrea was our best cheerleader. I was frequently grateful to her. I limped back to basecamp and plucked out as much gravel as I could from my wounds, then rinsed them in iodine water and wrapped them with gauze.

Caving involves a great deal of crawling. There was no way to get from one section of a cave to another without shimmying military-style on your elbows and knees through narrow tunnels. The gauze rolled off my wounds in minutes. During these four days I was going to continually reopen my wounds and it was going to hurt: this was simply going to happen and there was no way to avoid it. Something about the fact that I was the only one in this condition made it easier to do the difficult thing and not complain. My problem during the first phase had not been that I was weak. It was that I constantly compared myself to everyone else.

"You're not in competition with anyone but yourself," Robin told me gently when I lamented my slowness on the trail. That seemed like a sad position to me—to accept my deficiency with a cheerful attitude. But in the caves, it seemed like something I could do: opt for the better version of myself. Fake it until I made it. I crawled and bled, crawled and bled, and lived with it, without asking for sympathy.

Protocol was unique inside the caves. When we were out in the woods the woods were our bathroom. But we could not leave behind waste in the caves where it would never decompose. One night we camped next to a magical river; it was safe to pee in the river. Otherwise, we had to use one of two porta potties we carried with us throughout the expedition. Then we had to carry them.

Carrying the porta potty was a job even the most conscientious of our group avoided. They locked tightly and didn't smell, but we knew what was in there, and as the days went on their weight increased, and the only purchase for carrying was a slippery plastic handle. We took short turns with them before passing them off.

We exited the caves on day four with the porta potties at maximum, all of us coated in a thick layer of mud, blood staining the elbows and knees of my army jumper. I stripped off my jumper and tended my wounds and marveled at my "tenacity and spirit." Maybe these were qualities I could own after all. After we cleaned our gear and packed up, back in our regular hiking attire, we all stared with dread at the porta potties. Each of us had experienced the nauseating sloshing sound they made while being carried. The van that would take us back to basecamp waited for us across a vast field.

I did not want to carry an unwieldy and abundantly full porta potty across a vast field. But *could* I carry an unwieldy and abundantly full porta potty across a vast field?

"I'll carry one," I volunteered, to the surprise of my crew mates.

It was so heavy I had to stop and put it down every few steps. I was still trying to walk without bending my knees so the ever-forming scabs would stop breaking open. But by God I carried that box of horror all the way to the van. It didn't matter that when I reached the van my crew did not give me the round of applause I thought I deserved. I hadn't done it because someone told me to or because someone expected it of me. I'd done it because I'd decided to. It had been so much easier that way.

I entered the van and saw the empty seat next to Melissa. This was my designated seat now. I sat down next to her and pressed my leg against hers. She smiled her light beams at me.

It appears we are heading to a dovetailing of sorts, and we are. I could only become a better version of myself on Outward Bound by confronting my inner conflict:

by choosing the less comfortable, more perilous path of risking my social likability and turning to Melissa, I grew to accept the physical challenges on the trail with more ease. Or perhaps it was the other way around: once I accepted the physical challenges and took responsibility for my literal body, I could pursue the truth of my figurative heart. In either case, the escalation of my "tenacity and spirit" and my submission to some brand of love for and from a woman seemed to be leading, in tandem, towards a more evolved life, a reckoning. If my relationship yields a clean and happy ending, and if I also reach the top of the volcano because I choose to rather than because it was required of me, these threads will collide.

But of course, the true story is rarely that easy.

* * *

"That there's a real ending to anything," Carmen Machado writes in *In The Dream House*, "is, I'm pretty sure, the lie of autobiographical writing. You have to choose to stop somewhere." Memoir endings are merely offerings: they propose resolution to the reader when the writer's story goes on.

Strayed ends *Wild* in two ways. The material landing comes as no surprise: Cheryl reaches her destination, the Bridge of Gods. She places her hand on the bridge and gazes down at the Columbia river. "I had arrived. I had done it. It seemed like such a small thing and such a tremendous thing at once, like a secret I'd always tell myself, though I didn't know the meaning of it just yet. I stood there for several minutes, cars and trucks going past me, feeling like I'd cry, though I didn't." She orders an ice cream cone at the stand near the bridge and sits on a white bench to eat it, after which the tears finally come. Then she pushes her narrative into the future to arrive at the greater resolution: becoming the person she's wanted to be.

> *Thank you*, I thought over and over. *Thank you*. Not just for the long walk, but for everything I could feel finally gathered up inside me; for everything the trail had taught me I couldn't yet know, though I felt it somehow already contained within me. How…in four years I'd cross the Bridge of Gods with another man and marry him in a spot almost visible from where I now sat. How in nine years that man and I would have a son named Carver, and a daughter named Bobbi. How in fifteen years I'd bring my family to this same white bench and the four of us would eat ice-cream cones while I

told them the story of the time I'd been here once before, when I'd finished walking a long way on something called the Pacific Crest Trail. And how it would be only then that the meaning of my hike would unfold inside of me, the secret I'd always told myself finally revealed.

Twenty-six-year-old Cheryl is imbued with the potential of her future attachments, while simultaneously the Cheryl of the future is fortified by the incredible journey completed by her younger self. The threads of *Wild* meet as Cheryl and Strayed become one person.

By limiting her flash-forward to three or four paragraphs, and by rendering the future in sweeping strokes with no setting or context, Strayed maintains the solidity of the Pacific Crest Trail as her landscape. She tells us only what we need to know about how her life will go; the end of the trail is the end of the book. I thought about trying that for my ending here, too. But I think Cheryl Strayed was more of a realized adult than I was at the end of our respective expeditions. My journey had many false endings. I had a lot further to go.

FALSE ENDING ONE: LOVE WINS

I understood what it was to love a man, and I would again. But women tore me open in a different way from men. Or: women made me feel torn open in a different way from men, and it was always messier. My undergraduate self would need to reconcile this, to package it in a way that suggested logic. But from my current vantage point I understand that some things are not meant to be reconciled or ever understood. I had, and will always have, the capacity to love both women and men; there is no scale or measuring stick to explain or quantify the difference. Certainly, some variety of fear colored the way I linked with women. I once would have pointed at a fear of being gay, but really the way I experienced romance with women was roomier and more confusing, and the fear had something to do with these shaky parameters.

I knew this from my first encounter with H. Immediately after H. left my dorm room that night at the end of my first year in college, I paced furiously until the room ran out of oxygen, then walked the two blocks from my dorm to Dunkin' Donuts, the only business still open in the dead of night. Every nerve in my body was firing at random. The night air around me was charged. I wanted to open my mouth and evict the ragged scream that pulled at my sternum, but I couldn't identify what made me want to scream. At Dunkin' Donuts I spotted my friend Maneesh reasonably sipping coffee while bent over a textbook. I made friendly small talk with Maneesh as I listened to the much louder voice, my own, chanting in my head: *he doesn't know. He doesn't know.* The earth I knew had just been grabbed out of space and replaced with a different, more electrified sphere. We now lived in a world with a far less discernible bottom. And no one knew but me, and H. And the women like us.

Since the moment on the rug when I was fifteen years old, I had never disentangled lesbian desire from the aura of secrecy. Secrecy was part of its inconceivable draw—first the idea of it, and then the specificity of it. And it had never been as specific as it was with Melissa. It was a secret that Melissa's and my hands were in each other's hair in the blue dark of night as we slept in random places—the floor of a homeless shelter; a KOA campsite—on our road journey from North Carolina to Florida, where we were headed to canoe in the 10,000 Islands. It was a secret that we ran our fingers down each other's faces as we blinked at each other through the darkness in a group tent with mosquito netting at Everglades basecamp. We reached the end of our second month. Our new landscape was hot, muggy, and thick with mosquitos. The mown grass at Everglades base-camp was stiff against our skin. Drinking water came from jugs filled by taps, rather than dunked in rivers and sanitized with iodine. Beyond basecamp the Gulf of Mexico spread towards the limitless ocean. Mana-tees moved through the water, and somewhere close by, we continually reminded each other, alligators. Melissa and I took to sharing a tent with Caitlin and which-ever fourth person wanted to join us, and ran our hands over each other's bodies in their slick nylon casings. It seemed impossible that we'd ever locate a space to be alone, until a rare opportunity presented itself.

Before our canoeing expedition in the 10,000 Islands, which would include paddling in the open ocean, we were required to pass a swim test. Robin and Eliot dropped two cardboard boxes filled with oversized clothes from Goodwill on the dock. The main base-camp building was a large Florida-style house fronted on the water by piers. On the piers, and the rocky walls between them, oyster bars clung in dense clumps.

"Be careful of the oyster bars," was the first thing they told us. "Put on a shirt and pants over your bathing suit, then wade out into the water—don't kick. If you kick the oyster bars will cut your skin like razor blades. Wade out until you are clear of the dock and the wall. Then swim to the end of the pier, take off your clothes, hold them out of the water so we can see them, wait for our signal, then put on your clothes and swim back. When you return, remember to wade very slowly near the oyster bars."

I entered the water for the swim test with Allison, the girl in our crew who fell or injured herself nearly daily. The first thing Allison did was kick.

"I think I cut myself," she said, then sucked her teeth in pain.

"Let me see," I said. Allison tilted back and raised her leg above the water. A yellow gash of fat was visible within the slice across the bottom of her calf. It filled in fast and red with blood.

"I think you need to get out," I said, trying to conceal my alarm, and when she stepped onto the dock, the blood fell around her feet in a wide puddle before she could even scream.

While the rest of prepared to leave basecamp, Allison was taken to the hospital for stiches, then given her own tent to pitch on the grounds while her leg healed. She would sleep in this tent and do service at Basecamp while we paddled for the week.

That tent was still pitched when we returned from the 10,000 islands, and Allison was giddy to return to the group tent after a week of solitude, leaving a perfectly empty, perfectly available two-person tent erected across the grass from the corner of the grounds where everyone else would be sleeping.

At dusk I looked at the abandoned tent across the grass, then at Melissa. Melissa blinked back at me with her brown eyes. We gathered our sleeping bags in our arms and walked them over to the empty tent.

I kissed Melissa in the tent with my eyes closed. It was brief, this first kiss—a test kiss. I opened my eyes expecting to confront Melissa's fear, her hesitation, maybe her remorse.

Melissa's face broke into an enormous smile. An unfaked smile, an unbreakable smile. The kiss made Melissa...*happy*.

We kissed through that unbreakable smile until I broke it, pushing us both under the wave of giving into the want we'd built. My body was a pulled-back slingshot. I never thought I'd be so grateful for the flimsy walls of a tent. Much time would pass until we found another enclosed space in which we could strip off our clothes and have our bodies be privately together.

From there we stole moments when we could. In Mexico tents fell away to rented houses and hotel rooms, where we shared beds and lost our concerns for what our roommates knew. Weeks passed like this. Melissa liked to express her feelings through writing and would pass me letters at random moments. Sometimes these letters would mention her conflicted feelings, and her devotion to Edward, and soon that name was a short, skinny blade slid into my solar plexus. Edward! She'd known him for all of *two weeks*. How could she still be thinking about this dumb bearded hippie after all our crazy intense time together?

For the first time, I saw that this desire for women thing might not just be about bodies. It might just be about…*love*?

Melissa's smile, that first night in the tent, was an image that revisited me over and over—more than my relief upon seeing her display of uncomplicated joy, I was haunted by the idea that to me it had seemed so out of place. When confronted with its strangeness, I instantly tried to push through it, to carry her to the realm of bodies. To move with a woman directly from desire to happiness had never seemed an option. Of course, I had Edward to contend with—a foot against the door that led to us being happy together. There was also the unmistakable fact that Melissa and I inhabited different worlds managed by entirely different value systems and goals, and it was unlikely our worlds would merge beyond this wilderness. We were not building towards coupledom in any real way. But something new had unlocked, and had floated me out into something wet and floorless and terrifying.

What a leap! That had been my fear all along...*love*!

This might be a place to begin tapering my story towards its end. After establishing the necessary villains—homophobia, fear of change, fear of self—I might land at the place where two girls fell in love and triumphed over these villains. Love wins!

But Melissa did, of course, go back to Edward. As far as she was concerned she had never left him. Outward Bound ended and we went our separate ways.

I could still end this story here by positioning Edward as the villain—and believe me, in real life I did for a while. He might symbolize heteronormativity and its effortless control. It would be simple enough to suggest that while Melissa was really in love with me, the ease of being with a man, even one she barely knew, was too powerful to sacrifice over something confusing and impermanent and taboo. But perhaps the lesson, my "story," was that I now understood myself. I summited the volcano in Mexico with a clear new idea of who I was, courtesy of both Outward Bound and the brief love I'd shared with a girl whose motto was "share love and honesty." It is not untrue to suggest this. But this would be a short-cut truth.

I summited Izta, feeling great affection for my Outward Bound companions, and days later I suffered the loss of their daily companionship. Peter disappeared in the airport without saying goodbye to anyone, later explaining it was easier that way, and when he called me on my parents' landline a few days later, I was overcome with joy and missing him and all the people who had become like family. I drove to Providence to visit my college friends and slept at Valerie's house, crawling into bed in my fleece pants as if I expected the temperature to drop overnight, and woke up sweating, with rain pounding on the roof while I remained effortlessly dry; it was unparalleled luxury to enjoy the sound of the rain thumping on an impenetrable shelter above my head. My heart, after parting ways with Melissa, was a little bit fissured. But I was also electrified. I owned a new identity and had said goodbye to my old secret life.

I saw Melissa a few times in civilization, where we wore our normal clothes together for the first time—me in ribbed leotards and tight jeans and platform clogs, her in swirling skirts and unexpected decorations in her braids. I was now the owner of a pair of black Merrell Wilderness boots with fat blue laces and silver metal fasts. These boots were the first thing I bought upon my return. I wore them not because I was hiking a trail, but because of how they made me feel when I navigated the concrete walkways of the urban landscape that made the most sense to me. Later, I would lace them up them daily when I lived for a year in rural Costa Rica. These boots sit in my closet to this day. I love them.

I spent a week at Melissa's family home in Indiana, spending evenings playing double solitaire with her younger sister and her grandma, and once going with her sister to a fascinating high school party, since Melissa worked 8-hour evening shifts at Toys R Us in order to make money for the trip she was about to take with Edward. (Blade; solar plexus; repeat.) She visited me in New York a few times. We wrote letters. We drifted apart. I spoke to her on the phone during the writing of this book. She works as a massage therapist in the mountains of Colorado and is married to a man. I'm sure she is equally unsurprised by the life I made—writer, teacher, marrying a woman and settling in a city. The love and caring we nurtured for each other is still there. It is quite a thing, to know someone so well from having endured something so difficult, so long ago. To answer the phone and within moments think, *You: I know you. And I know exactly who I am when I talk to you.* How wild.

FALSE ENDING TWO:
IN SEARCH OF RELUCTANCE

The truth was I had chosen Melissa to fall in love with first not despite her reluctance, but because of it. I felt how far I could descend, so I chose women who would not allow themselves to abandon gravity with me. The floors of the women I chose were solid and impenetrable: they were loyal to other partners; they had no interest in identifying as gay; they had no desire to commit. As the years went on I unknowingly proved my agenda again and again, beginning only a few months later when I studied abroad in Seville, Spain.

The pattern was exact. Our program director explained to us that the professor of the Cervantes seminar was a genius in his field, and also regularly chose one American student each semester to court. We should understand the latter thing about him, and if we had a problem with this we should probably not request the class. "And if Luis does hit on you," she said wryly, "you should not think you are special." I had already enrolled in the Cervantes class and was eager to crack my Spanish and English editions of *el Quijote*; the word "genius" excited me. When Luis invited me to a party at his apartment, I arrived to find myself the only student in a small group of professors from the University of Seville. Luis was handsome, charming, and brilliant, but arrogant. He fed me Ferrero Rocher chocolates and red wine and drove me home and we made out in his miniscule red car. He retrieved me the following day for an outing. It was easy. It was fun. It went on. In class, we argued vehemently. One day he lost his patience with the class when he learned that not one of us had read Virgil. I suggested the importance of reading contemporary books, citing Toni Morrison as an example, and he spat out, "How can you"—red-faced, spittle flying—"compare Toni Morrison—to VIRGIL!" That we constantly challenged each other in the classroom fueled our push-pull attraction. With men, there always seemed to be something I had to fight against, so battles felt normal. Opposition was built into the cultural stamp of our difference, the chasm of privilege that could never be bridged.

But the appeal of the push-pull with Luis quickly gave way to my more active interest: the closeness

I'd been cultivating with a fellow American student, Margaret. I demoted my thing with Luis to flirty, scholarly friendship. Margaret was one of those magnetic people everyone loves instantly and I loved her instantly. She had terrible fashion sense, confirmed by an awful haircut she'd gotten just before I met her at a local beauty school that left her curly brown hair unsure of which way to point. She was indiscriminately kind, spoke excellent Spanish, and fell into a romance with me in a way that was both full-throttle and bursting with denial. "I don't think I'm gay," she said, as we made out in every doorway in the Los Remedios neighborhood where I lived with my Spanish family. She loved me, and that was easy for her to say and to show when we were alone. But she could not bring herself to think of me as her "girlfriend." In terms of social priorities she ranked me as an equal to her many friends. When men hit on her in front of me, she flirted back—not because she wanted anything from them, but because they wanted her to. I slouched miserably across a bar table and watched her hold hands with our friend José Luis, a well-meaning engineering student who was obviously in love with her and on his way to getting burned. "Why do you have to do that?" I asked later. "What?" she asked, wide-eyed and innocent, no matter how many times this happened. "José Luis is my really good friend!" I pushed her and pushed her to acknowledge what we were: in love, *in a gay way.* By the time she finally caved, I'd been beaten down by frustration.

I would continue, over the years, to push the responsibility for my emotional experience onto others, until finally I handed the whole basket of my self-worth to a woman whom I knew couldn't carry it—because no one can carry that for someone else for long—and then I watched her drop it and stayed wrecked for two years. How much easier it was to blame someone else for my vexations, rather than to fully embrace the genuine self-reliance I'd gone searching for on Outward Bound. I made it someone else's job to pull up a place for me to stand, to render me stable. I had to be the architect of my own solid floor, of course. But I couldn't do it until I could.

Eventually, I met a woman who was unhesitant to enter into a relationship with me. I was unhesitant to enter into a relationship with her. We had a beautiful wedding. But I can't end there.

Because the marriage wasn't happy—it was my ultimate false ending.

Because even if it had been happy, I've already written a memoir that ended with marriage.

Because women memoirists do this all the time, too often, and we need to understand resolution on different terms. We need to locate and articulate a more involved intricacy in our outcomes. I've already done my part in perpetuating the notion that marriage is a woman's ultimate landing spot, her happy ending. Now I want to, and have to, do something else.

THE END OF THE TRAIL

Giving birth to my first child was the end of my trail. Not becoming a mother but the physical act of birth. The baby was not irrelevant, of course, but in the aftermath of wrangling him into the world, everything clicked into place, not because of the baby but because I'd birthed him. My hand touched the bridge. The human I was linked hands with the human I wanted to be.

The body holds, hangs onto, wisdom for longer than the mind understands. It stores memories in muscle. The knowledge my body had wrapped up after Outward Bound and put in storage for when I'd need it, particularly about not comparing myself to anyone else, erupted from its packaging when I became serious about yoga. Without the physical lessons I accumulated through a sustained yoga practice—trusting my body and accepting it as it was, landing in breath, finding stillness in chaos, understanding the difference between the conversation in my brain and the experience of my body—I may not have planned an unmedicated birth. When my wife and I devised our "birth plan," I added the requisite clause about accepting intervention in the form of pain medication or caesarean section if the situation called for these things. But I had already decided I would not need those things. I was going to have my baby the hard way. The Outward Bound way. No special climbing shoes or extra-cushioned sleeping pads. I was going off trail through the thicket. My pack was stocked with all the proper objects.

My due date came and went. I figured I may as well grade my final exams and record my grades for the semester because this baby wasn't coming. Perhaps I'd be pregnant in perpetuity. I sat at my desk and did arithmetic, converting letter grades into numerical grades and posting final grades on the registrar's page, slowly acknowledging the clenching in my abdomen. Moments after I entered my last grade and texted my doula "I think I'm in labor," I was face-down on the floor, clawing at the carpet.

The landscape I visited during those twelve hours of unmedicated labor was the alone-est terrain I'd ever known. I'd counted on the pain progressing gradually, but I arrived at the hospital slammed with close-together contractions that never quit. I entered the birthing room and said to the nurse—whom I was sure had rolled her eyes at my "natural birth" plan—"I'm not sure I can take this for very long." Those were the precise words my mother uttered to her OB when she entered the birthing room to have me. Her OB replied, "Oh, you're having this baby any minute," and he was correct; my parents had barely made it to the hospital. This was the response I was soliciting, but instead the nurse said in a sing-song voice, "You don't have to feel this pain. You don't have to feel anything at all." Her tone suggested not feeling pain was an excellent idea. In my mind-bent state I perceived her as an adversary trying to tempt me into committing a malicious act. I did indeed need to feel this pain. It was part of the deal. I was going to do this thing as my body was built to do it.

During those hours my wife and my doula were in the room with me, and the midwives and nurses came and went. But I had never been more alone. When I closed my eyes I saw my body moving though a thick, blue-black shallow liquid in a black space. Above the black water, I watched sentences float in white type-writer font:

I changed my mind.

This was a bad idea.
I don't really need a baby.
How can I get out of this?

Then I would remember that quitting was out and be swallowed back down by the black water. I recalled all the times I'd abandoned things, particularly writing projects. How easily I'd turned away from them, all those things I'd ditched. This was much harder than writing! I wanted desperately to ask for help, but no one could help me beyond transmitting me medical attention or comfort from some remote corner of the universe. The solitude of giving birth was a shock administered to me at regular intervals as I worked to move my baby down. I was finally alone on the trail.

The episode from Cheryl's hike that unnerved me the most was not the scene in which the two male hunters come upon her and stare her down in a way you know could go dark very quickly. Though that scene was harrowing, it was almost expected (*Given the statistical realities, all women live all the time under the shadow of the threat of sexual abuse*), and Cheryl thankfully avoided physical harm. No, it was the scene when snow obliterated her footpath—the trail she'd come to trust, the thing that told her she moved in the right direction. She'd have to navigate by faith.

The snow, which she thought she'd bypassed, surprises her as she comes around a muddy bend in the trail. No footprints dot the vast white expanse: no previous hiker has cut a path for her. She guesses her direction, takes her first step. Soon she's cold and shivering, "skittering over the top" of the snow in some places, in others, her feet "crash[ing] through, sometimes forming potholes up to my knees." But her snow-soaked, burning ankles "worried me less than the fact that I couldn't see the trail because it was buried beneath the snow." Spending days in this state of nagging concern, with the heightened threat of weather, with no companion there for reassurance, was a kind of harrowing far beyond anything I'd experienced as a hiker. Being alone with the *not-knowing*.

I'd been very lost in the wilderness before, and I'd been lost enough that I threatened to run out of food, but I was always disoriented and hungry in the company of others. Bickering and swearing at each other while lost on Outward Bound was a luxury in comparison to Cheryl's need to "walk on" with no insurance that she was not driving herself deeper into a trail-less wilderness, even risking death. But she walks on, of course she does, until she arrives at the safety of a road. Afterwards, she "dreamed of the things that could have happened but didn't. Skidding and sliding down a treacherous slope and off the side of a cliff or crashing into the rocks below. Walking and never coming to the road, but wandering lost and starving instead." I would have panicked the minute I stepped into the snow, I thought, if I were to face these fears alone. I would have turned back, called for help, quit. But what if I were to let myself panic—what would happen if I'd been in her situation, panicked, and then…what? Maybe I could walk on in the face of terror, too. As scared and in pain as I was in the birthing room during the birth of my first child, this was what I'd been looking for all along: navigating a harrowing, unknown landscape, *alone*.

How much closer together are my contractions going to get? I asked my midwife. How long was this going to take? I begged my doula. They couldn't tell me because they didn't know. I staggered from the bath to the bed to the birthing ball, again, again, and again.

I walked my labor for twelve hours, most of them hellishly stalled at 8 centimeters dilation. When I felt I'd done all I could and the contractions began hitting without pause ("double-peak" contractions!), I decided it was time for an epidural. My son came forty-five minutes later. When the nurses took him out of the room for tests, I reached for my laptop and started

THE WANTING WAS A WILDERNESS

writing. I wrote out my birth story. A few weeks later, I considered the two books I'd been writing slowly over the years, both of which were "not far from done." Why weren't they done? If I could make a baby I could certainly make a book. What had I been hemming and hawing over? I finished both books while my son was still a baby, and sold them.

Something shifted in my creative writing classroom around this time, too. My students began taking more risks in their work. I read their essays and stories with awe and interest, their raw, vulnerable, detailed stories of their young lives. After a decade of teaching creative writing at this college happily enough, the classroom environment had a new power—we were truly all in it together, this figuring-out-life thing. I knew I could do it, finish a daunting writing project, fight back the desire to give up on myself, and understand something about myself through writing. So I knew they could do it too. I believed in them with all my heart. It was the strangest, most natural thing.

As anticipated, I'd loved being pregnant, giving birth, nursing babies, and being a mom. We had a second child. I toured for my books. After the third child arrived and my writing time shrunk to near nothing, Fiction Advocate approached me to write a critical memoir for their new series, a work of literary criticism with room to explore a book of my choice as I pleased. I chose *Wild* from their list, thinking a short and focused book was a project I would enjoy and could manage while mothering three young kids.

While everything else had clicked into place for me, my marriage, especially after our third child was born, had grown tense. Intimacy had vacated our union long ago, and the differences between our hopes for the future cast a taller shadow over us each day. When the kids slept, I hid away in my office and escaped into the world of *Wild*, Sugar, and Cheryl Strayed. I didn't want to think that my marriage was unhappy. But I also knew it was deeply unhappy. I read Sugar's advice and read and re-read *Wild*. In a few months I wrote a solid half of a solid book. As I tried to figure out what I wanted to say by the end of the book—my message, my "story"—one of Sugar's lines continued to nag me: *Be brave enough to break your own heart.* It was one of her famous appeals. I wasn't sure how it applied to me yet, but I had a sinking feeling it did.

In an interview with the *Paris Review*, James Baldwin said, "When you're writing, you're trying to find out something which you don't know. The whole language of writing for me is finding out what you don't want to know, what you don't want to find out." I was writing a book about a book about self-reliance, and being true to oneself, and claiming both of those things on some level. But there was one way I was not being true to myself or anyone else and it would stay that way as long as I stayed in my marriage, and the more I wrote, the more of a problem this became. A silent internal debate played on a loop. *Our marriage is fine in so many ways. We are great parents together. I love her family. But she doesn't seem to even like you! She yells at you literally every day. And there are things you're never going to like about her. It's just a bad match. It's fine! It's not THAT bad. We can last a while longer. I'll deal with this later. This doesn't mean I'll never know love again. The kids the kids the kids.*

One "fine" night when my wife and I were barely speaking, I sat curled up on an armchair reading *Tiny Beautiful Things* while my wife rinsed dishes in the kitchen and the older kids watched a video and the baby slept. I read Sugar's words:

> You cannot convince people to love you. This is an absolute rule. No one will ever give you love because you want him or her to give it. Real love moves freely in both directions. Don't waste your time on anything else.

I watched my wife move over the sink. She hadn't been reluctant to commit to a relationship with me, but she'd always been reluctant to be in love with me. I'd been trying to convince her to love me from the beginning, and she would have said she did; but she and I had different ideas about love. I thought to myself, *I am not living an authentic life.* How could I write a book about living an authentic life, finding a "tractor beam of truth" to light the way in writing about life, if I couldn't do it myself? I turned to the faces of my children, blued by the TV screen. I had to be brave enough to break my own heart.

One afternoon in early summer, when the baby was about to turn one, my wife appeared in the doorway of my home office, her face tense with anger. She had stored up an enormous amount of resentment over a work trip I'd taken to Cuba and had barely looked my way since I'd returned, and if she did, her face looked like this. She'd come to argue. I felt unusually calm.

"I can't live like this," I said quietly. She stopped, confused.

Out of my mouth streamed a steady flood of all the truths I'd confined to my head, some of them since our third child was born, some since our earliest time together. All the things that meant our marital alliance was beyond fixing, that if I uttered would cause an irreparable crack in the marriage. The reality was I still didn't want a divorce, because I couldn't imagine how we could ever force the logistics to work, and being apart from my kids half the time was an unbearable proposition. But I had to tell the truth.

We made it through the summer. By fall our separation was underway.

One landscape from my time on Outward Bound recorded itself permanently in memory for its majesty: the peak of Table Rock Mountain. Table Rock, a tall, skinny mountain in the Linville Gorge of the Pisgah National Forest in North Carolina, was an easy summit for us, straight uphill but only a mile from the base. At the summit, we clustered together and ate bread and cheese as our leaders toyed with ropes and carabiners at the rock's edge. We were surrounded on all sides by a sheer drop. It was quiet except for wind and the scuffling of rocks and leaves. The vista was limitless. Rolling mountains stretched out around us on all sides and faded out into the horizon. Looking south we could see the vertical cliffs of the Chimneys, where we'd been climbing in our seatbelt-webbing harnesses the past few days. Climbing, you touched your nose to the grey rock and felt the brush against your skin and the cliffs seemed immense; now our view was the full mountain in miniature. I felt how small I was.

Eliot called us over one by one to a spot around the low-growing trees, out of sight of the rest of the group. I bit into my bread nervously. The view was our prize for the hike, but we'd really come here to jump off a cliff.

Bets were taken on who would chicken out. The drop was one hundred and fifty feet. The assignment was to poise sitting at the lip of the cliff, gently clench the rope woven through the carabiner attached to our harness, position our dominant hand to "break," and then—face first—jump.

Eliot called my name. I walked slowly through the wind, feeling at the knots in my harness and clicking the carabiner hooked at my pelvis a compulsive few times. I met Eliot at the edge. Far below us those who had already jumped meandered in the brush, distant and doll-like, their faces too mini to make out.

I sat on the side of the cliff and felt the wind whistle around me.

"You have to do it," Eliot said, quietly and simply.

"I know," I said, quietly and simply.

He squatted in ready position, the ropes that led to my hand looped around his waist to secure me. He was there to immobilize my ropes if for any reason I lost my grip, but I would be responsible for belaying myself down, slowly letting out my own ropes.

Eliot waited. I looked out into the empty air. Jumping into it was unfathomable. But it was also something I had to do.

I leaned forward. I pressed my heels against the rock. I jumped.

If there was a moment of peak aloneness on Outward Bound, it was this rappel down Table Rock Mountain. Once I'd pushed through the terrifying beginning I found myself dangling reasonably by my rope, my hand supporting my weight almost without effort. Eliot had disappeared over the lip of the cliff. It was a long way down to the friends who waited. It was just me and my rope and the wind and the rock and one hundred and fifty feet. There was work left, but there was also incredible peace. I pushed off with my feet and swung out on the rope, letting it out bit by bit. The distance wasn't the hard part. The hard part was the having to choose its beginning.

I jumped out of my family structure, the container that held my life. The journey to solid ground was a long one. But I knew I could reach that ground. Shapes and colors blurred around me as I plummeted. When my feet hit dirt I was free.

And then I returned to my desk and finished the book that was meant to be written, the truest truth I could offer you.

REFERENCES

Works Mentioned

Steve Almond. Introduction to Cheryl Strayed. *Tiny Beautiful Things: Advice on Love and Life from Dear Sugar*. New York: Vintage Books, 2012.

Maya Angelou. *I Know Why the Caged Bird Sings*. New York City: Random House, 1969.

Sven Birkerts. *The Art of Time in Memoir: Then, Again*. Minneapolis, Minnesota: Graywolf Press, 2008.

Bill Bryson. *A Walk in the Woods: Rediscovering America on the Appalachian Trail*. New York: Broadway Books, 1998.

Bill Bryson. *Notes from a Small Island*. New York: William Morrow, 1995.

Isak Dinesen. *Out Of Africa*. New York: Modern Library, 1952.

Jessica. "James Frey's Author's Note of Fury." *Gawker*, gawker.com/152435/james-freys-authors-note-of-fury.

Jordan Elgrably. "James Baldwin, The Art of Fiction No. 78." *The Paris Review*, 9 Aug. 2019, www.theparisreview.org/interviews/2994/james-baldwin-the-art-of-fiction-no-78-james-baldwin.

Michel Foucault. *The History of Sexuality. Volume I, An Introduction*. New York: Vintage Books, 1990.

James Frey. *A Million Little Pieces*. New York: Random House, 2003.

Garden and Gun Editors. "Dorothy Allison on the Necessity of Making Readers Uncomfortable." *Literary Hub*, 22 Nov. 2019. lithub.com/dorothy-allison-on-the-necessity-of-making-readers-uncomfortable/.

Elizabeth Gilbert. *Eat, Pray, Love: One Woman's Search for Everything across Italy, India and Indonesia*. New York: Penguin, 2006.

Elizabeth Gilbert. "Confessions of a Seduction Addict." *The New York Times*, 24 June 2015, www.nytimes.com/2015/06/28/magazine/confessions-of-a-seduction-addict.html.

Vivian Gornick. *The Situation and the Story : The Art of Personal Narrative*. New York: Farrar, Straus, And Giroux, 2002.

Lucy Grealy. *Autobiography of a Face*. Boston: Houghton Mifflin, 1994.

Elizabeth Greenwood. "Eat, Pray, Love Like a Badass: Cheryl Strayed, the Oprah Author 2.0." *The Atlantic*, 8 Oct. 2012, www.theatlantic.com/entertainment/archive/2012/10/eat-pray-love-like-a-badass-cheryl-strayed-the-oprah-author-20/263317/.

Ernest Hemingway. *A Moveable Feast*. New York: Scribner, 1964.

Kathryn Harrison. *The Kiss*. New York: Random House, 1997.

Kathryn Harrison. *Thicker Than Water*. New York: Random House, 1991.

Ann Hood. "Every Story is Two Stories." *The American Scholar*, 12 Jan. 2015, theamericanscholar.org/every-story-is-two-stories/#.XCfD1i2ZN-U.

Denis Johnson. *Jesus's Son*. New York: Farrar, Straus, and Giroux, 1992.

Lacy M. Johnson. "On Likability." *Tin House*, 11 Oct. 2018, tinhouse.com/on-likeability/.

Alden Jones. *Unaccompanied Minors: Stories*. Milwaukee, Wisconsin: New American Press, 2014.

Mary Karr. *Lit: A Memoir*. New York: HarperCollins, 2009.

Mary Karr. *The Art of Memoir*. New York: HarperCollins, 2015.

Michiko Kakutani. "'Amaze Me,' Mother Said, So That's What She Did." *The New York Times*, 5 Nov. 2009, www.nytimes.com/2009/11/06/books/06book.html.

Maxine Hong Kingston. *The Woman Warrior*. New York: Vintage International, 1976.

John Krakauer. *Into Thin Air*. New York: Villard Books, 1997.

Carmen Maria Machado. *In the Dream House: A Memoir*. Minneapolis, Minnesota: Graywolf, 2019.

Catharine A. Mackinnon. *Toward a Feminist Theory of the State*. Cambridge (Massachusetts): Harvard University Press, 1991.

Frank McCourt. *Angela's Ashes: A Memoir*. New York: Scribner, 1996.

Daniel Mendelsohn, "But Enough About Me." *The New Yorker*, 2017, www.newyorker.com/magazine/2010/01/25/but-enough-about-me-2.

Sara Nelson, "Interview with Cheryl Strayed." *O: The Oprah Magazine*, http://www.oprah.com/spirit/Wild-by-Cheryl-Strayed-Cheryl-Strayed-Interview#ixzz43HQMyojz

George Orwell. *Down and Out in Paris and London*. New York: Harcourt, Brace, 1950.

Cheryl Strayed and Robert Atwan. *The Best American Essays 2013*. Boston: Houghton Mifflin Harcourt, 2013.

Cheryl Strayed. "Heroin/e." *Doubletake*, April 1999.

Cheryl Strayed. "The Love of My Life." *The Sun Magazine*, www.thesunmagazine.org/issues/321/the-love-of-my-life.

Cheryl Strayed. *Tiny Beautiful Things: Advice on Love and Life from Dear Sugar*. New York, Vintage Books, 2012.

Cheryl Strayed. *Torch*. Boston: Houghton Mifflin, 2005.

Cheryl Strayed. *Wild: From Lost to Found on the Pacific Crest Trail*. New York: Alfred A. Knopf, 2012.

Adam Rowe. "Traditional Publishers Are Selling Way More Non-Fiction Than Fiction." *Forbes*, 30 Aug. 2018, www.forbes.com/sites/adamrowe1/2018/08/30/traditional-publishers-are-selling-way-more-non-fiction-than-fiction/#f90a49756d0e.

Paul Theroux. *The Kingdom by the Sea: A Journey around Great Britain*. New York: Washington Square Press, 1992.

The New York Times. "The 50 Best Memoirs of the Past 50 Years." *The New York Times*, 26 June 2019, www.nytimes.com/interactive/2019/06/26/books/best-memoirs.html.

Jerald Walker. *The World in Flames: A Black Boyhood in a White Supremacist Doomsday Cult*. Boston: Beacon Press, 2017.

Jeanette Walls. *The Glass Castle*: *A Memoir*. New York: Scribner, 2007.

Tara Westover. *Educated: A Memoir*. New York: Random House, 2018.

Lex Williford and Michael Martone. *The Touchstone Anthology of Contemporary Nonfiction: Work from 1970 to the Present*. New York: Simon & Schuster, 2007.